D028644.6

BACKROADS & BYWAYS OF
WASHINGTON

BACKROADS & BYWAYS OF
WASHINGTON

Drives, Day Trips
& Weekend Excursions

Archie Satterfield

The Countryman Press
Woodstock, Vermont

We welcome your comments and suggestions.
Please contact
Editor
The Countryman Press
P.O. Box 748
Woodstock, VT 05091
or e-mail countrymanpress@wwnorton.com.

Backroads & Byways of Washington
ISBN 978-0-88150-825-3

Book design by Hespenheide Design
Map by Paul Woodward, © The Countryman Press
Interior photos by the author unless otherwise specified
Composition by Chelsea Cloeter

Published by The Countryman Press, P.O. Box 748, Woodstock, VT 05091

Distributed by W. W. Norton & Company, Inc., 500 Fifth Avenue, New York, NY 10110

Printed in the United States of America

10 9 8 7 6 5 4 3 2 1

To the memory of
Chester and Pearl Bell of Washtucna,
the best friends of my life,
whose decency and good cheer were the reasons
I chose to make my home in Washington.

Washington

Contents

Introduction

Not long ago at a dinner party in Bellingham we realized that none of us had been born in Washington. North Dakota, Missouri, Ohio were represented on our birth certificates but not Washington. That only rated knowing smiles because for most of us, America has a westward tilt that made us roll, like balls in a pinball machine, across the prairies, plains and mountains to the West Coast. But what did surprise us was that we all arrived in the Puget Sound basin during the same season, autumn, and that each of us had identical emotions on first seeing Puget Sound. Even though we knew nothing about the Sound's wet climate or the long, dark winters, still we felt that we were coming home.

I came home almost by default. I had been going to universities in the Midwest and working on a wheat farm near Washtucna the previous three summers. In the process I became friends with Chet Bell, the man I worked for, and, in fact, he became the best male friend I ever had. I doubt that a day has gone by since his death in the late summer of 1980 that I have not thought of him and his wonderful wife, Pearl. So I loved the open, hot-and-cold, sunny rolling plains of Washington's wheat country and cast about for a way to remain in that region. Chet and I talked about becoming partners in farming, and I was sorely tempted. But the love of writing took precedence, and my wheat-country friends were disappointed that I chose the University of Washington in Seattle ("the coast," as everyone there called everything west of the Cascade Mountains) over Washington State University in Pullman. As much as I loved the wheat country, I never regretted the move. Indeed, the Puget Sound basin quickly became home—it was love at first sight.

Today, when I drive down off Snoqualmie Pass toward Puget Sound, only some of that initial shock of recognition remains. But on that September afternoon many years ago I was surprised at how beautiful Puget Sound is. Instead of the naked ocean of the coastlines of the world, Puget Sound has the beautiful Olympic Mountains for a backdrop, and in the foreground are the many low-lying islands, plus all the activity common in sheltered waterways: the ferryboats running back and forth between the mainland and the islands and the Olympic Peninsula, the several kinds of fishing boats, the tugboats towing barges or log rafts, the hundreds of sailboats and powerboats, and cargo ships arriving from or departing to exotic names on the maps of Asia.

Seattle then was not the architecturally exciting place it is now. Its tallest building was Smith Tower. No trees lined the streets. The waterfront was dreary. The city had perhaps half a dozen good restaurants, and only one or two could be called outstanding. But in the words of every real estate salesman in the world, it had that magical ingredient: location, location, location.

Because the Cascade Range divides the state, not only in terms of geography and climate but also in political outlook, Washington seems to have a mild, manageable form of schizophrenia: One side bears absolutely no resemblance to the other. Nearly everything is different; different scenery, different crops, and different politics. Western Washington is known nationally for being one of the most liberal places in the United States, while eastern Washington has a decided conservative tilt. Yet I don't recall ever encountering the bitterness and hatred that often occurs in the rest of the country when liberals and conservatives rub against each other. Courtesy is not a forgotten virtue in this far corner of the country.

A caveat is in order on two topics, food and lodging.

First, the food: I have never completely accepted the growing opinion or belief that the Northwest has earned its wings (buffalo or otherwise) in the world of cuisine. More and more, we see and hear references to Northwest cuisine. That is a stretch to this old Northwesterner. I don't think the region deserves such a highfalutin name for its food, especially when you compare it with what I have always believed that only two ethnic foods are original enough to earn the right to be called a cuisine: French and Chinese. Italian comes very close, in my opinion, and North African is an also-almost-ran. But to label food prepared in the Northwest a cuisine is, in my opinion, pushing the definition beyond its limits.

What is this food that some call "Northwest cuisine"? It is, specifically, the cuisine of Oregon, Washington, Alaska, British Columbia, and the southern Yukon. It reflects the region's ethnic makeup, including elements from Asian and Native American traditions. Seattle's Pike Place Market is a hub of this culinary style; Portland and Vancouver are also influential. Salmon, shellfish, and other fresh seafood, often smoked or grilled on cedar planks; game meats such as moose, elk, or caribou; mushrooms, berries and other small fruits, potatoes, and wild plants such as fiddleheads and young pushki are commonly used ingredients. Great emphasis is placed on fresh ingredients, prepared simply, but, unlike other cuisines, there are various recipes for each dish and none is considered more correct than another, a fact that has led some food writers to question whether there really is a distinct Northwest cuisine.

The second topic is lodging. Where I sleep is of little or no consequence to me. If the room and the bedding are clean and the lock on the door works, and if the bathroom is en suite rather than somewhere down a creaky corridor, I'm content. But many people consider lodging a major part of the travel experience, and the fluffier the bedding, the better, and if the orange juice at breakfast has been freshly squeezed, little else matters. I have traveled with people who read guidebooks constantly, compulsively, while ignoring beautiful scenery and colorful small towns. My personal attitude toward this kind of travel is not favorable, and while I hope many people will read this book, I hope they will plan their trips around the landscape rather than where to eat and sleep. If you're going to be away from the large population centers—and what else is a backroad?—either bring your own food in assorted coolers, or simply eat what the locals eat. A food writer once won my respect when he said that when he is in doubt about what to order in a café attached to a car repair shop, he always orders a cheeseburger and French fries. And for lodging, don't waste the day worrying about where you'll sleep that night. You're not in the Gobi Desert. A large town is never far away.

In general, I have arranged these trips in a clockwise manner, beginning the book in the Seattle area and returning across Puget Sound at the end. Some of these trips are not much more than small diversions from driving the interstates and other boring main roads across and up and down the state. I am assuming that many other travelers like to wander aimlessly occasionally, frittering away a few hours of their lives in search of pleasant surprises and pleasant memories.

Most of these trips are on true backroads, but a few—especially the along the Columbia River, the Yakima Valley wine district, the North Cascades Highway, and US 101—tend to stretch the definition of backroads. I beg your forgiveness in advance because those trips are among the best Washington has to offer. And I also beg your forgiveness for selecting some roads that are really, really backroads. Some of these routes don't even have a place to buy a cheeseburger, and they certainly do not have B&Bs with fluffy down comforters and pillows piled high on the beds. But I think you will enjoy these remote, seldom traveled roads as much as I do.

—Archie Satterfield

Slow Road to Bellingham

Estimated length: 71 miles
Estimated time: 3–4 hours

Getting there: Take I-5 north from Seattle to Exit 199 at Marysville. Follow Marine Drive west under the freeway and through the Tulalip Indian Reservation to the community of Warm Beach, then north to Stanwood. Continue north on Pioneer Highway to Conway, then go left/west on Fir Island Road, following the main winding route La Conner. From La Conner, follow the La Conner–Whitney Road due north across WA 20 to the Bayview–Edison Road to the tiny town of Edison. About a mile further, at Bow, take WA 11 north on Chuckanut Drive to Fairhaven, on the outskirts of Bellingham.

Highlights: This backroad includes beaches, sloughs, parks, dairy farms, small dressed-up theme towns, fields of tulips, tourist towns, rugged coastline, and excellent country restaurants.

This route is one of the favorites with shunpikers because parts of it follow the shoreline of Puget Sound as closely as highway engineers permit, adds about an hour to the trip and perhaps 30 miles while giving you a welcome relief from the clenched-teeth syndrome suffered by so many drivers on I-5.

Going north, begin at Exit 199, marked Marysville-Tulalip, and go west beneath the interstate into the Tulalip Indian Reservation. (By the way, it is pronounced *two-lay-lip,* not *two-la-lip* as I pronounced it on arrival in Washington.) The road generally follows the shoreline, which has a few sloughs where fishing boats and tugs are parked picturesquely. Clusters of expensive waterfront homes line some of the bluffs and bays, most of which were built on land leased from the Tulalip tribe. The Tulalip were one of the first tribes in Washington to establish gambling casinos to increase tribal income, and with that income in recent years the tribe has been buying back land that was taken from them by the treaties of the mid-nineteenth century. Thus you will see a shopping mall surrounding the casino and hotel on the west side of I-5.

Beach access is very limited on the reservation but the marine and forest scenery are striking and you'll find an occasional convenience store. However, shortly after leaving the reservation, and 13 miles from the interstate, you will come to Kayak Point County Park, which has one of Puget Sound's nicest county-owned parks. The point juts out into the sound at the base of a steep bluff and the 670-acre park has broad lawns for sports, a 300-foot long fishing pier, a good clamming beach, picnic tables, a shelter that can be reserved for a fee, campsites, and a boat launching area.

From Kayak Point the road ambles through second-growth timber and between suburban homes and quickly goes through Warm Beach, a small community that got its name from the shallow bay where the sun warms the saltwater enough for comfortable wading and swimming. Soon the road swings back inland against the bluffs, with enough elevation to avoid being inundated at low tide. To the west, the land is flat and diked and has occasional drainage ditches to keep brackish water from covering crops. As with nearly all flat land between Seattle and the Canadian border, fat Holsteins with udders almost dragging the ground graze between milking times. This is some of the best dairy farming land in America.

Stanwood is the first town of significance after leaving Marysville. It is primarily a farming town with some allowances for tourism and the growing population on Camano Island just west of town. As islands go, Camano isn't much because it is separated from the mainland only by a small ditch-like passage spanned by a short bridge. Nearly the entire island has been turned into building lots and it is a popular second-home and retirement community.

The main route, which now is WA 530, continues north from Stanwood across rich soil created by the estuary of the Skagit River. Over the centuries the river has swung back and forth over several miles, dumping it load of silt to create some of the richest farming land in the Northwest. The estuary is composed of several branches of the river that have been diked to prevent nearly annual flooding. These efforts are only marginally successful and in spite of the prospect of having everything soaked if not washed away, people have insisted on building their homes on this land, as flat as an airport runway with an elevation of only inches above sea level. Nearly all houses are built on stilts or high mounds of dirt and rock, but they are still flooded often. Thus, almost every winter the newspapers and television stations send crews to the Skagit Valley to report on the latest disaster, which could easily have been prevented by working the land but living on high ground somewhere nearby.

The Pioneer Highway bumps into Interstate 5 at **Conway,** but this trip takes a sharp left at Conway and continues across the farmland. Conway is very small, with a large and slightly rickety old wooden building that serves as a farmers' market during the long growing season; three and sometimes four crops are grown on the land here, thanks to the moderate climate and rich soil. An occasional new building appears in Conway, but still the most striking building is the Lutheran Church on the western edge of town.

The stretch from Conway onward is the most popular part of this trip because the farms here grow bulbs—tulips, daffodils, and irises—thousands of acres of them, and when the tulips are blooming in the spring the roads are clogged with cars, tour buses, bicycles, joggers, and Volkssport walking-club members. It is one of the Northwest's most beautiful sights and sales of photographic paper rise dramatically during this period.

The road between Conway and La Conner is a typical farm road; its route is dictated by property lines

A scattering of beautiful churches is part of the Skagit Valley's charm.

and local geography, so be prepared for corners rather than curves as it goes between farms and across ditches and arms of the Skagit River delta. At one point it gains perhaps 200 feet in elevation along Pleasant Ridge, and gives a great view of the fields with Mount Vernon off in the middle distance and the Cascade Range forming the horizon. Several beautiful homes line the ridge, including at least one bed-and-breakfast in a Victorian home.

La Conner is one of those tiny towns that began its life as a fishing and farming village, but grew into something quite different. It is near the southern end of Swinomish Channel, a shallow and narrow saltwater channel that separates Fidalgo Island from the mainland. Like Camano Island, very few residents of Fidalgo consider it a true island, although legally speaking it is. La Conner was discovered many years ago by Seattle-area artists, including Guy Anderson, who liked the isolation, the casual and inexpensive lifestyle, and the scenery that inspired some of their best artwork. They painted the flat farmland with mountain backdrops, the fishing boats, and the fog that often hangs on the land and turns the few trees into spectral visions. The novelist Tom Robbins lived here long before he became famous and a cult figure, and some of his novels and essays describe the area vividly.

Today La Conner is one of the most popular destinations for visitors, from both far and near. To step aside from editorial anonymity, I don't understand why it is so popular. About all you see there now are other tourists and gift shops. Perhaps that represents both charm and security for most travelers. Having said that, I find myself going there often, usually to meet one of my women friends for a meal. Note to guys: Women love La Conner.

Twenty-some years ago, when La Conner was emerging from its slumber as a fishing town and being reborn into a trendy tourist destination, somebody in the town's government was stricken with a wonderful pun. At that time Renault, the French car manufacturer, was in partnership with America Motors Corporation and they introduced a car built for export to the U.S. They named it Le Car. So the city fathers of La Conner bought Le Cars for their small police force that would never, ever go in pursuit of a felon. Le Car. La Conner. Get it?

The **Valley Museum of Northwest Art,** in the old Gaches Mansion, has one of the best collections of artwork by artists who lived in La Conner, and works by other regional artists are on display.

Each spring when the flowers are in bloom, the roads around La Conner are jammed with traffic and the smarter visitors bring their bikes, park in Mount Vernon, and tour the Skagit Flats on their bikes. Several farms sell flowers and will ship anywhere in the world. The tourist offices in Mount Vernon and La Conner have names and addresses of the shops. A favorite is **West Shore Acres,** just north of La Conner along Swinomish Channel. The 1896 Victorian farmhouse there is surrounded by thousands of tulips of every color and size. Bring a camera. The site contains a 1.5-acre flowering bulb display garden.

From La Conner this route heads due north on the La Conner–Whitney Road, crosses busy WA 20, and goes on north to Bayview, where the Bayview State Park overlooks Padilla Bay, the enormous petroleum refinery at March Point, Anacortes, Guemes Island, and the other San Juan

Each spring hundreds of visitors wander through the tulip gardens at West Shore Acres near La Conner.

Islands. Shortly after leaving Bayview, the road ducks inland over a hill and through tall timber, then emerges with views north across the small Samish River and Samish Bay to the Chuckanut Mountain.

The road ends at a T-shaped intersection where a left turn will take you out to Samish Island, another island barely separated by a ditch. Samish is a small, slender island almost completely covered with homes. The right turn takes you on the main route to the small town of **Edison,** where you can stop for a snack or a drink in one of two taverns. You can buy specialty food items, such as rare cheeses and hard-to-find wines, at **Slough Foods.** You will also see a store that handles either antiques or interesting junk, perhaps both. Another popular food stop is the **Farm-to-Market**

Chuckanut Drive is something of a short (10 miles) version of California's Highway 1 as it clings to the side of steep mountains between Mt. Vernon and Bellingham.

Bakery, also on Edison's main drag (actually, the town has only one "drag"), which attracts bread lovers from all over the region. A *Seattle Post-Intelligencer* food writer, Hstao-Ching Chou, once wrote of Edison: "Edison may begin and end in a glance, but it sure knows a thing or two about feeding an appetite."

About a mile further is WA 11, the famous **Chuckanut Drive.** You can go straight across WA 11 and climb over Bow Hill to I-5 if you want, but unless you're in a terrific hurry, shun that idea. Turn left, or north, at this intersection. You'll be glad you did. A good restaurant, the Rhododendron

Café (described below), is at the intersection, plus a store that stocks antiques and general "old stuff."

The route runs across more flat land until it reaches the shoreline at the foot of Chuckanut Mountain. Here it crosses a bridge, and suddenly you are following the edge of the mountain above the shallow water that turns into tideflats at low tide. Chuckanut Mountain rises sharply here and for that reason it is a popular launching pad for hang gliders. Be prepared to see them settling slowly back to earth, like giant dandelion seeds, in the open field east of the road.

Chuckanut Drive was Washington's first highway built for scenery alone. It clings to the face of the mountains something like California's Highway 1. Because the mountains along here are so steep, few homes have been built. Burlington Northern railroad runs a track along the base of the mountain just above the waterline, and AMTRAK uses these rails for its Vancouver-to-Seattle passenger service.

Three good restaurants have been in business on Chuckanut Drive for many years. The first is the **Rhododendron Café,** back at the junction of the Bow Hill Road and Chuckanut Drive. As is the case with the other restaurants, the "Rhody" Café has been here more than 20 years and has enjoyed great popularity all that time. The second one, **Chuckanut Manor,** is on the flats immediately south of the mountainous part of the drive. It is the most spacious of the restaurants and the most low-key, partly, one suspects, because the building is so large and rambling. In addition to the fine restaurant and large bar, it also features two B&B bedrooms upstairs. The **Oyster Bar** is roughly in the center of the mountainous part of the drive, where it clings to the steep cliff and overlooks Puget Sound and the Taylor Shellfish Farms directly below, where you can stop to buy a wide variety of fresh shellfish. Toward the end of the drive is **Larrabee State Park,** which has good picnic areas, nice walks along the rugged shoreline, and overnight camping. Established in 1915 as Washington's first state park, Larrabee is also one of the largest, spanning 2,683 acres from sea level to 1,940 feet elevation, and occupies most of the west side of Chuckanut Mountain.

Chuckanut Drive ends rather suddenly at a traffic light in Fairhaven, a Victorian village that is part of Bellingham. The decidedly mundane Interstate 5 is only a short distance away.

IN THE AREA

Accommodations

Alice Bay B&B, 11794 Scott Rd., Bow. Call 360-766-6396 or 800-652-0223. This B&B has a private beach with lots of waterfowl, and great scenery across the flats to mountains on both the east and west horizons. Web site: www.alicebay.com

The Heron Inn & Watergrass Day Spa, 117 Maple St., La Conner. Call 360-466-4626 or 877-883-8899. The 12-room inn and spa has private baths, some fireplaces, and some jetted tubs. Breakfast is included.

Hotel Planter, 715 First St., La Conner. Call 360-466-4710 or 800-488-5409. This restored old hotel has 12 rooms, accessible by stairs, and is in the downtown area. The rooms have handmade furniture. There is a hot tub in the courtyard.

Katy's Inn, 503 S. Third St., La Conner, Call 360-466-9909 or 866-528-9746. Situated atop a hill with views down the Swinomish Channel, where boats go to avoid Deception Pass, this B&B has four rooms with private baths.

La Conner Channel Lodge & Country Inn, 205 N. First St., La Conner, Call 360-466-1500 or 888-466-4113. This is the only waterfront hotel in La Conner and it features rooms with private balconies, fireplaces, weekend wine-and-cheese reception, and breakfast.

Attractions and Recreation

Valley Museum of Northwest Art, 703 S. 2nd St., La Conner. Call 360-466-4288.

West Shore Acres, end of Downey Rd. Call 360-466-3158.

Dining

Calico Cupboard Café & Bakery, 720 S. First St., La Conner. Call 360-466-4451. Breakfasts and lunches, vegetarian and "lite" entrees. Serves Northwest wine and micro beers.

The Taylor Shellfish Farm on a strand below Chuckanut Drive has been a source of seafood for many years.

Chuckanut Manor, 3056 Chuckanut Dr., Bow. Call 360-766-6191. In addition to the fine restaurant and large bar, Chuckanut Manor also has two B&B guest rooms upstairs. The owners are avid anti-smokers and will levy a $50 surcharge if you light up in the inn.

Kirsten's Restaurant, 505 S. First St., La Conner. Call 360-466-9111. Intimate dining with Northwest dishes emphasized. Lunch served Fri., Sat., and Mon.; dinner Mon. through Sat. Closed Sun.

La Conner Seafood & Prime Rib House, 614 S. First St., La Conner. Call 360-466-4014. The name says it all. Open daily from 11:30 a.m.

Nell Thorn Restaurant, 205 Washington St., La Conner. Call 360-466-4261. Contemporary and classic cuisine. Lunch Tues. through Sat., dinner every night.

Oyster Bar, 2578 Chuckanut Dr., Bow. Call 360-766-6185. The Oyster Bar specializes in seafood, as its name indicates, with an occasional beef dish finding its way onto the lunch and dinner menus.

Rhododendron Café, 5521 Chuckanut Dr., Bow. Call 360-766-6667. The "Rhody" has a regular Northwest-style menu featuring seafood and locally grown vegetables, but it changes each month to highlight cuisines from around the U.S. and the world, including Italian, Spanish, Indian, Middle Eastern, and so forth. Web site: www.rhodycafe.com.

Other Contacts

Kayak County Park, 15610 Marine Dr., Stanwood. Call 360-652-7992.

La Conner Chamber of Commerce, 606 Morris St., La Conner. Call 360-466-4778.

Larrabee State Park, 245 Chuckanut Dr., Bellingham. Call 360-766-8300.

CHAPTER

2

Mountain Loop Highway

Estimated length: 52 miles
Estimated time: 2–3 hours

Getting there: From Everett, take US 2 to WA 9, go north to the Lake Stevens junction with WA 92, and take it to Granite Falls. In Granite Falls, follow the Mountain Loop Highway signs to Darrington.

Highlights: Some of the good reasons for making this trip are seeing Granite Falls—the waterfall just outside the town of the same name—on the South Fork Stillaguamish River, and Granite Falls Fishway, beside the falls. Also, there are numerous picnic areas and campgrounds, trails for short hikes, secluded lakes, a four-mile hike to the ghost town of Monte Cristo, ice caves, bald eagles in the winter, and the boulder-filled Sauk River.

After many years of miners and shopkeepers struggling to the mining camp over riverbeds and rough trails, funds were allocated in 1936 for a proper road through the Cascades foothills to the gold-mining district around Monte Cristo. The road, soon nicknamed the Mountain Loop Highway, opened in 1941, just in time for World War II to begin. Almost immediately it was closed, sometime in 1942, for the remainder of the war. The highway closes most winters because of flooding and it usually reopens in the spring. But this was not the case between 2003 and 2008. A severe windstorm hit in 2003, and before the damage could be repaired and the road reopened, more windstorms hit in 2006 and 2007. At last it reopened in 2008, and the towns along the route had a large celebration on the opening day of June 25.

This 55-mile loop trip seems designed for Sunday drives. From late June through October few places in the Puget Sound basin are more popular. Fortunately it has so many picnic areas, campgrounds, and one- or two-car-sized turnouts that it can absorb a lot of people before you start feeling crowded.

This trip is one of the first I took into the heart of the Cascades shortly after my arrival in Washington, and any doubts I may have had about my choice of a new home were dispelled after this drive. My love for this trip even survived two bad experiences on it. The first was my first-ever camping trip; I had slept out and ate cold pork-and-beans out of the can while working in wheat harvest in the Great Plains and on cattle ranches in Colorado and Wyoming, but I had never slept out just for fun. My first such experience was on the shore of Bear Lake with people who couldn't tolerate solitude. They treated my solo strolls with deep suspicion, and stared at me for long moments when I returned. The only way I could get a few minutes of alone time was to go out into the middle of the lake on a poorly constructed raft that would support only one person. I felt both foolish, while sitting on the rickety craft, and very put-upon.

The next episode occurred just after my first child was born. The car broke down and while I was looking at the engine, the seat of my pants ripped out. Almost at the same moment, my wife spilled a chocolate milkshake on her white shorts. I wrapped a sweater around my waist to cover my bare bottom and she draped the baby's blanket over her stained shorts while we walked back to the Verlot store, made a phone call to a friend in Everett, and waited for him and his wife to go to an auto parts store and bring us a fuel pump. It was a very long afternoon. But we never blamed it on the Mountain Loop Highway, and have since gone back many times.

The first miles of the drive between Everett and Granite Falls are rather disappointing now because the route goes through the urban sprawl that is slowly munching away at the Cascade foothills. Bear it in good cheer, if you can, because once you reach **Granite Falls,** the landscape becomes Mount Baker–Snoqualmie National Forest and the sprawl of new homes is left behind.

A mile north of the town of Granite Falls you will cross the high bridge over the falls of South Fork Stillaguamish River. Stop here for a walk down the mountainside along the 540-foot-long walkway along the **Granite Falls Fishway,** built many years ago to enable salmon to migrate past the falls. For many years, this fish ladder was the longest in the world.

The paved road follows the course of the river, locally known as the Stilly, and fishermen are always out working the riffles and pools in search of rainbow, eastern brook, sea-run cutthroat, and steelhead. This probably isn't the most appropriate time to go on this rant, but after trying many, many times and suffering primary hypothermia—not to mention embarrassment for being so stubborn and probably stupid—I arrived at the conclusion that steelhead are a fish invented by some evil person as a fairy story to tell newcomers to the West Coast, much like snipe hunting in other parts of the country. Make note of this, dear reader: I have lived in the Pacific Northwest many years and have never seen a steelhead. Never.

Where was I? Oh yes.

Every turn of this road, and there are many, gives you a new and equally beautiful view of the river, its steep valley, and the forested mountains on either side. Numerous trails lead off the main road to viewpoints, trailheads, or small lakes tucked away above the valley.

Four evergreens stand like sentinels in the snow along Highway 9.

This first portion of the loop along the Stillaguamish came into being after a substantial gold and silver discovery was made back in the Cascades in 1889. The discovery was named Monte Cristo, and it was so promising that a railroad was built from

Puget Sound to the mine. All of this activity caught the attention of prominent East Coast investors, including the Rockefeller family, and as a result the Rockefellers and assorted partners built the town of Everett at the western end of the Monte Cristo railroad. Then the Great Northern Railroad came through Everett and the town's future was secure, even though the crash of 1893 and the recession that lasted until 1897 dealt it a hard blow.

The Monte Cristo mine created a lot of work in the area and the town of **Monte Cristo** grew up around it, along with Silverton, a bedroom community for the mine. Many traces of the mining years remain, including some machinery and other equipment. There is a catch, though: Monte Cristo is at the end of a four-mile hike.

From the Monte Cristo turnoff, the Mountain Loop Highway takes a sharp left turn to the north and is gravel the rest of the way to Darrington. The road soon joins the **Sauk River** and follows its course northward. Numerous campgrounds have been built along this route, and you'll have several choices of trails to hike back into the national forest and the Henry M. Jackson Wilderness. Glacier Peak, the volcanic peak that is seldom mentioned because it isn't visible from any road, isn't far from the Sauk River, and you can hike out of the river valley on several trails for good views of the peak.

Darrington is one of the more interesting towns along the base of the Cascade Range because it began as a logging town where most of the residents were self-proclaimed Tar Heels. They moved to Washington from North Carolina to work in the timber industry, and they brought with them their customs and their bluegrass and country music. Each summer the town hosts a bluegrass festival in July that brings tourists and musicologists from all over the West.

At Darrington you have a choice of continuing north on the paved WA 530 to Rockport on WA 20, the North Cascades Highway, or turning west on WA 530 to Arlington and back to I-5. The road to Rockport goes through forests and past streams and lakes while the route to Arlington generally follows the Stillaguamish River as it goes through a more populated area, past several farms and campgrounds.

Lodging and dining are basic along this route. Unless you are camping, you'd be better served by shopping for picnic ingredients at grocery stores, and planning to eat and stay overnight in larger towns.

IN THE AREA

Other Contacts

Verlot Public Service Center, 33515 Mountain Loop Highway, Granite Falls. Call 360-691-7791.

Darrington Ranger Station, 1405 Emens Ave. N., Darrington. Call 360-436-1155.

The border between the U.S. and Canada is not only the longest international border in the world, it is also one of the most benign. The actual border is the ditch between two-lane highways in each country.

3

Highway 9 to Canada

Estimated length: 100 miles
Estimated time: 2–3 hours

Getting there: Take WA 9 from Woodinville straight north to the Canadian border at Sumas.

Highlights: This much slower, bucolic alternative to Interstate 5 goes past farms and lakes and crowds the foothills of the Cascade Range. It meanders along the edges of large towns—Snohomish, Marysville, and Mount Vernon—and through well-tended small towns such as Clear Lake, Sedro Woolley, Deming, Nooksack, Everson and Sumas. It is seldom more than ten miles from Interstate 5 and most of the major towns for the first half of its route. It makes a good alternate route to and from Vancouver, British Columbia, particularly if you are not interested in driving through downtown Vancouver and across the Lions Gate Bridge to North and West Vancouver.

Washington shunpikers love Highway 9 because it parallels I-5 from the Seattle area all the way to British Columbia, and offers a flavor of times past when people more often than not used their cars for pleasure. It has the advantage of being close to the main north–south arterial of I-5, and you can drive the whole length or only certain segments that appeal to you. For example, at Snohomish the highway crosses US 2, one of the last coast-to-coast highways that takes you over the Cascades via Stevens Pass.

Highway 9 crosses several other highways that can take you to larger towns nearby. It crosses SR 92 at Lake Stevens, which leads back to the Cascade foothills town of Granite Falls, and beyond to the Mountain Loop Highway (see chapter 2). The next crossing is WA 530 at Arlington, which leads to Rockport with an alternate turnoff onto the northern end of the Mountain Loop Highway. It is only a few miles further that it crosses Highway 20, the North Cascades Highway, and WA 542, the Mount Baker Highway.

This route begins just east of Woodinville and bisects the suburbia that keeps sprawling farther and farther north and east. Actually, you won't miss much, other than this depressing collection of houses and apartment buildings covering rich farmland, and extremely slow traffic because of a series of traffic lights, if you don't bother finding WA 9 until Arlington. From Arlington north it is a more honest country road. It is also crookeder and narrower, has less traffic, and you get to see bucolic scenery and smell bucolic smells, especially in the spring when dairy farmers are spreading the natural fertilizer produced by cows. The odor from this fertilizer is so strong and prevalent that Whatcom County requires purchasers of rural land to acknowledge that they have been warned about the odor.

Rather than cutting straight across the good farmland, WA 9 winds along the edges of hillsides overlooking the valleys, and sometimes it climbs over a low hill to the next valley. Occasionally it even makes a 90-degree angle, as if the highway engineers wanted to avoid disturbing some Norman Rockwell scene or declined to cut through a productive farm.

After going through some heavy timber, past privately owned tree farms and around sharp curves, you will reach Lake McMurray, which is mostly a residential area with modest summer cabins sprinkled among the more substantial homes. The next town is Clear Lake, a small village with a few false-front store buildings and a Quonset hut that probably dates back to the end of World War II, when these buildings were sold off as surplus.

You'll also note that many houses along here stand almost against the highway blacktop. The owners didn't build that close to the highway by choice. At one time the homes had real yards and were several feet back, but as the highway was widened, the front yards were gobbled up by the blacktop.

The highway continues on past Mount Vernon, missing it by a mile or two, then goes through Sedro Woolley and crosses WA 20, the North Cascades Highway. Sedro Woolley came by its unusual name in a typically mixed-up bureaucratic fashion. Locals named it Cedro, Spanish for "cedar," because so much cedar grew in the area. The post office accepted the name, but the bureaucrats anglicized the spelling to *Sedro*. A man named Woolley built his own town nearby and of course you know what happened: the two merged. Sedro-Woolley has the headquarters of the **North Cascades National Park,** and several gift shops and art galleries.

For the remainder of the trip to the Canadian border, the landscape alternates between flat land used for dairy farming and berry growing, and trees. You'll see several nurseries along the way that grow Alberta spruce, which grows into perfect cone shapes. As an aside, all Alberta spruce trees we see now are children of a single "sport," or mutation, from another tree found in Alberta. The oddly shaped branch found growing on that tree was cut off and propagated, creating a whole new species of tree.

But be forewarned: Highway 9 from Sedro Woolley to the Canadian border at Sumas is the route of choice for Canadian trucks, RVs of all types, and travelers from everywhere east of Vancouver. The highway is a great shortcut for them. A look at a map of Washington and British Columbia will show that Highway 9 permits them to avoid roughly 100 miles of extremely busy highway and will save them the grief of stopping-and-starting and lurching their way through Vancouver traffic. Be prepared to share the two-lane highway with heavy traffic, often consisting of the semis that seem to grow in length with each passing year. Australia is known for its 4-6 trailer "road trains," and it seems that North America is trying to catch up. Fortunately accidents are a seldom thing, but meeting a truck that consists of two or three trailers being towed behind can be a startling event.

The first hills of the Cascade Range loom almost overhead from time to time, and on clear days 10,778-foot **Mount Baker** will suddenly appear through the trees or between the hills. Before Mount St. Helens became active again in 1980, seismic activity began on Mount Baker and people assumed that if any of the Cascade volcanoes would erupt, it would be this one. However, Mount St. Helens took over in a big way and Mount Baker returned to its slumbering.

Wickersham and Van Zandt still exist after a fashion but are faint shadows of towns. Acme is a bit more of a town and has a wonderful country store and a café. **Deming** is considerably larger, in spite of being on the very, very small Nooksack Indian Reservation. Like most other tribes across the United States, the Nooksacks built a casino that attracts thousands of gamblers, including daily chartered buses from British Columbia.

Lawrence still shows on maps but it is nothing more than a church and a cemetery. Everson and Nooksack are jammed together and are a bit larger than the other towns between them and Sedro-Woolley, but Sumas,

Winter often brings deep snow on Highway 9 because arctic weather sneaks down the Fraser River canyon in British Columbia and dumps loads of snow across the border.

on the U.S.–Canada border, is the largest town on the route since Sedro-Woolley. Sumas, however, is mostly a border town, a place for Canadians to come across to buy cheaper gasoline and to shop. Many Canadians who do business in the States rent post office boxes in the border towns to avoid the delays caused when mail must cross back and forth across the international border. There are probably some advantages related to not having to pay duty on goods shipped to the U.S. and taken across the border, but good neighbors do not tattle on each other.

Whatcom County, Washington's farthest northwest county, is famous for its agriculture. The black soil is very deep, the growing season long and the summer climate generally mild. So the county has thousands of acres of berries: blueberries, strawberries, and particularly raspberries. The county accounts for nearly one-half of the raspberries grown in the United States, and one privately owned agricultural company grows more than 25 percent of the national output. Seed potatoes are another extensive crop you'll see along WA 9.

While the international boundary with Mexico continues to create problems, few countries in the world are better neighbors than the United States and Canada. The U.S. has continually irked Canada for various reasons. Paramount among them is simply ignoring Canada because it is so peaceful. The boundary between the two countries is one of the longest in the world—from the Arctic Ocean down to Washington, then all the way across the continent to Maine and New Brunswick. This boundary is not patrolled on a regular basis nor does it have guard towers, barbed-wire fences or searchlights. It is supposedly the longest border in the world without these unfortunate signs of boundaries. A caveat is required at this point, though: Since the events of September 11, 2001, an assortment of sensory equipment has been installed along the border. You may not see it from the road, but agents in both countries can see you as you peer into the trees and at the utility poles. It is okay to look, but don't test them by darting across the border. You will regret it if you do.

For a look at this situation, take Halverstick Road west just outside Sumas and follow it to Northwood Road, then turn right (north) and go to Boundary Road, which soon turns left (west). Boundary Road is a two-lane blacktop road that has farmhouses and barns on the south side, and a ditch on the north with utility poles planted in the ditch. Across the ditch is another two-lane blacktop road, and it has houses and barns facing south. It may take you a moment to figure out this mirror image. It often does, but when you see a mailbox adorned with the Canadian maple leaf you will understand: The ditch is the international boundary.

In theory, you are subject to a substantial fine if you walk across the ditch into Canada without clearing customs. But in practice the authorities do not interfere with the friendships that normally develop between the neighbors. One benefit of this tolerance policy is that the farmers on both sides keep an eye on the border and would report anything suspicious they happened to see.

Since September 11, 2001, even this benign border has become more difficult to navigate. You are now required to show a passport, and traffic is often backed up as much as a mile as agents go about their work. Occasionally, but only occasionally, the crossing at Sumas on SR 9 will take only a few minutes. The alternative, if you live in the area and often visit Vancouver, is to apply for a Nexus pass, which is good at the Blaine crossing only. It allows you to cross the border both ways in a special lane that moves very rapidly. But it is no help on SR 9.

As with the Mountain Loop Highway, overnight lodging and dining options are limited here. The best choices are found along I-5 and along the coast of Puget Sound on Chuckanut Drive (see chapter 1).

Boaters make a run for it through Deception Pass, where the tides bring fast and furious currents.

CHAPTER

4

Across the State on Highway 20

Estimated length: 440 miles
Estimated time: 3 days minimum

Getting there: Begin on US 101 on the northeastern Olympic Peninsula, just after it swings south after following the Strait of Juan de Fuca. WA 20 heads north off US 101 and ends, more than 400 miles later, at the Idaho state line.

Highlights: This two-lane state highway visits the Victorian town of Port Townsend before hitching a ride on a Washington State Ferry to cross Puget Sound, and then goes up Whidbey Island, crosses Deception Pass, meanders across the tulip fields of the Skagit Flats before crossing the Cascade Mountains to the Western-themed town of Winthrop. From there it traverses the Okanogan Highlands through the gold-mining town of Republic before finally heading south beside the Pend Oreille River to end in Newport, on the Idaho state line.

Almost any time you see a list of the prettiest country highways in America, WA 20, better known as the North Cascades Highway, will be on the list. If not one of the top ten, it will at least be in the Honorable Mention category. Other highways may be more spectacular but you will be hard pressed to find a highway with so much variety of scenery. It is born in the rainy

Olympic Mountains and crosses the state by going over mountains, across deserts, and through the wide-open scenery of north, central, and eastern Washington.

WA 20 is an offspring of US 101, born at the southern end of Discovery Bay on the Olympic Peninsula. There it heads north through the forest for about 15 miles to **Port Townsend,** that most Victorian of all Washington towns. Port Townsend began with very high hopes: Its citizenry was convinced it would become the San Francisco of the Northwest, and indeed, it was the port of entry for all foreign vessels. Several governments had their consulates in mansions along the top of the steep bluff overlooking the town and the entrance to **Puget Sound.** Unfortunately, the town's future fizzled when the railroad arrived and stopped its westward movement in its tracks on the eastern shores of Seattle and Tacoma. This left Port Townsend little more than an isolated appendage, and before long all national and state offices moved to the railheads. It would be nearly a century before Port Townsend came into its own, this time as a trendy place for Seattleites and Californians to escape the urban rat race for what they hoped would be a small-town atmosphere. It is still a small town, but when people migrate they almost always bring their attitudes and personal requirements with them. Consequently, Port Townsend has remnants of imported attitudes, especially from California, that include a fondness for trendiness and a faint attitude of superiority. A large number of Californians have settled along the shores of Puget Sound and in the assorted islands, in many cases because they were sailing north and discovered the beauty of the sheltered waters of Puget Sound. Many parked their sailboats, quit their jobs (or, if they were self-employed, packed up their offices), sold their homes, and went north to where they had left their boats.

Port Townsend probably hosts more festivals, concert series, and special and annual events than any other town in the state, perhaps more than some cities four or five times its size. The town has proven the wisdom of the famous line in the film *Field of Dreams*: If you build it, they will come. Many of these events are held at the two former military posts built to protect the entrance of Puget Sound. The most widely used is **Fort Worden,** on the outskirts of town, and Fort Flagler, a short distance away on Marrowstone Island, is a determined runner-up. Long after World War II ended and fears of a Cold War invasion evaporated, the forts were abandoned and turned over to the state parks system. Thanks to some inspired leadership in the parks system and in Port Townsend, both outposts were turned into performing arts centers with frequent concerts, music festivals, and assorted conferences. Fort Worden, by far the busier of the two because it is in Port Townsend's backyard, soon became by far the most popular. An enormous Quonset hut became a foundry for sculptors, and the old barracks and officers' quarters were turned into basic hotels and apartments so they could be rented to visitors.

Downtown Port Townsend is a conglomerate of upscale gift shops, trendy Northwest-cuisine restaurants, real estate offices, and specialty food shops. It is the kind of town that women love and most men tolerate to be with the women they love.

Places to stay and eat will be discussed briefly at the end of this chapter, but one hotel deserves to be singled out for the unusual story of how it got its bathrooms. **The Manresa Castle** on the south hill overlooking town began as the home an early entrepreneur built for his wife. Then it became a nunnery and then quickly became a training college for Jesuits. This lasted from 1925 until 1968, and it was named Manresa Hall in honor of the Spanish town where Ignatius Loyola founded the Jesuits. When the Jesuits left, it was turned into a hotel with only three bathrooms in the entire building for around 40 rooms.

Fast forward to 1982, when Port Townsend and Fort Worden were chosen as the location for the movie *An Officer and a Gentleman,* which starred Richard Gere, Deborah Winger, and Louis Gossett, Jr. There was a problem: The film crew's union contract called for considerably more bathrooms than the measly three that had been deemed sufficient until then. They had already booked every motel and B&B in town and needed more. So the film producers advanced enough money for the Manresa owners to install the required number of bathrooms. And that is why there are 43 bathrooms in the hotel today, up considerably from the original three.

From Port Townsend, WA 20 hitches a ride on a **Washington State Ferry** across Admiralty Inlet, which is the entrance to Puget Sound, and about half an hour later arrives at Keystone on Whidbey Island. During the summer months it is strongly suggested (not yet required) that you make reservations on the Port Townsend–Keystone ferry. The ferry is small and during the summer months the wait can be a very long one, so reservations (no deposit required) guarantee you a spot on the ferry rather than having to almost camp in line in the holding area.

This is one of the more interesting of the Washington ferry rides because all ship traffic to and from Puget Sound is funneled through the narrow inlet and sometimes the large ships seem to be staging a parade as they steam through. Also, the tides flow rapidly through the inlet, almost like a swift river, and when the tides are unusually low some of the ferry schedules are suspended because the Keystone landing area on Whidbey Island is too shallow. No matter the time of year, as the ferry comes in to the Keystone dock, you will see RVs of all types, plus tents, on the park's beach below the bluff.

When you drive off the ferry at Keystone, turn left rather than right so you can visit **Fort Casey State Park,** which is on the bluff above the small bay where the ferry lands. Fort Casey, one of the three original guardians of Puget Sound, was the recipient of the last intact ten-inch "disappearing rifles." Actually 10-inch cannon, these odd weapons were used for harbor defense between the two world wars. When the cannon were fired, the recoil caused them to swiftly swing backwards and down out of sight so they could be reloaded in safety. The sighter stayed aboard the cannon for the whole procedure, getting a wild ride and sometimes a perfect black eye from the recoil, which drove the sighting scope into his face. These cannon were originally teamed with a set of enormous mortars, but the mortars were removed shortly after the first test firing; the concussion broke windows for miles around and gave children nightmares for weeks. It was much like riding out frequent Mount St. Helens eruptions.

Fortunately these enormous mortars weren't used long at Fort Casey on Whidbey Island. Windows rattled and broke each time it was fired in practice, never in anger.

The original cannon at Fort Casey were sent to military-surplus heaven. Those on display today were removed from a military base in the Philippines and given to the fort. They obviously don't work anymore, but a walk around them will give you an idea of how Rube Goldberg could have been credited with inventing them.

Window-shopping is encouraged in Coupeville.

State 20 heads north up **Whidbey Island,** at 47 miles the longest island in the state. For a brief time about thirty years ago Whidbey was believed to be the longest island in the lower 48 states, the result of a cockeyed court decision that said Long Island, New York, wasn't actually an island. Apparently the decision still stands, although hardly anyone pays any attention to it. After all, if Long Island is completely surrounded by water, and you don't have to be a cartographical genius to see that it is, how could it be a peninsula? Leave it to the courts to make such a decision without laughing aloud.

Some Whidbey Islanders still push the "longest" claim but for the most part they have had to curtail their crowing.

Before the highway enters any sign of urbanization, it comes to one of the most unusual land-management plans in the nation: **Ebey's Landing National Historical Preserve.** It was the first such preserve in the nation when it was created in 1978 and it encompasses 17,500 acres that include 18 working farms, about 400 historical structures, native-grass prairies, uplands, woodlands, saltwater lagoons, and hedgerows, fences, and roads dating from the 1850s. Ebey's Landing also includes two state parks, several miles of trails, and the town of Coupeville, the second-oldest town in the state. For the casual visitor, the preserve is no big deal because it is farmland and some beach property looking normal but what you see there today is what your children, grandchildren and each succeeding generation will see. This is because the original mission statement said the preserve was intended to protect "a rural community which provides an unbroken historic record from nineteenth century exploration and settlement in Puget Sound up to the present time." The preserve is managed now by an entity called the Trust Board, which is composed of representatives from the National Park Service, Washington State Parks, Island County, and the Town of Coupeville.

The prairie and preserve were named for Isaac Neff Ebey, the first non-Indian to settle on Whidbey Island. He moved there in October 1850, and immediately wrote his wife back in Ohio to pack up their two young sons and their belongings and join him. He also tried to talk his relatives and good friends into coming out, and several crossed the plains and mountains to join him. Ebey was to live seven more very active years on Whidbey Island, becoming a player in territorial affairs. He was also prosecuting attorney, worked on separating Washington and Oregon into separate territories, and was appointed by President Franklin Pierce to collect customs. In this capacity he moved to Port Townsend and made it the official port of entry to Puget Sound.

This all ended in 1857 when a party of Haida Indians from Canada's Queen Charlotte Islands paddled their enormous canoes south along the British Columbian coast and down to Whidbey Island in search of an important white man to murder in retaliation for the murder the previous year of a Haida chief by white men. They were after Dr. John Kellogg, who lived near Admiralty Head. He was away, so the Haida went to the next white man's home, that of Ebey. They called him outside and shot him dead

Coupeville's historic business buildings are part of the small town's allure.

on his doorstep, then beheaded him and left carrying the head.

Three years later, Captain Charles Dodd of the Hudson's Bay Company traded six blankets, three pipes, one cotton handkerchief, six "heads" of tobacco, and "1 fthm. Cotton" for Ebey's head. By that time most of the head was gone but the skin, ears, and most of the hair remained. These gruesome remains were interred in the Ebey family cemetery on a bluff overlooking Ebey's original home.

Highway 20 arrives in the historic town of **Coupeville** at a traffic light. It is a lovely, still-small town, and the second oldest settlement in the state; Steilacoom was founded a year earlier, in 1849. Coupeville was built along the south shore of Penn Cove, a long, narrow, and picturesque inlet that almost cuts Whidbey Island into two islands. Most of Coupeville is strung along a street that follows the waterfront. Shops line both sides of the street, and a few restaurants are on the saltwater side. Many of the buildings on

The two-span bridge is one of the favorite scenes in the state, and Deception Pass State Park, seen here, is the state's most-used park.

the water side were built on stilts so that you are either dangling out over the saltwater, or it feels like you are. A long pier juts out into Penn Cove with a former warehouse at the end. Now the pier has at least three shops and cafes, plus large outdoor artwork.

When you leave Coupeville, consider driving along the Penn Cove shoreline so that you can see the large **mussel farm** in the cove, which is a series of floats with rope networks dangling below to provide a home for the mussels until they become food for humans. Take Madrona Way from the downtown area. Also on this route is the venerable Captain Whidbey Inn, one of the oldest hotels on the island, nestled among several madrona trees with terrific views across the cove. One corner of the main building is occupied by a restaurant and bar called **Ship of Fools,** which opened in 2009 with a typical Northwest menu featuring mussels from the farms in Penn Cove.

Madrona Way rejoins Highway 20 at the end of the cove and leads you into the largest town on Whidbey Island, **Oak Harbor.** This town's main source of income and population is the naval air station just north of town.

In one of those meteorological oddities, even though most of Whidbey Island is as rain-soaked and overcast as the rest of Puget Sound, the Oak Harbor area gets more sunshine and less rain than any other place around, which is why the Navy built a large air station here. Oak Harbor has all the amenities of a large town, including several national discount stores, good restaurants, and a wide selection of lodging.

Continuing northward you arrive at the north end of the island, which ends in a dramatic fashion. First the highway enters **Deception Pass State Park** and you are instantly aware of how the island once looked, with the dense forest almost hiding the sun, and the underbrush of salal and assorted berry vines so thick that walking through the forest would be almost impossible. An added attraction is the low stone-and-pole fencing built along the two-lane highway by Civilian Conservation Corps (CCC) during the Great Depression.

This is the state's most popular park, and you will understand why when you cross the Deception Pass Bridge. The saltwater at the bottom of the 180-foot drop below the bridge is in almost constant motion as the tide rushes back and forth through it, often at 8 to 10 knots, creating whirlpools, waves, and backwashes. Although the bridge is usually spoken of in the singular form, it is actually two bridges because they connect to tiny Pass Island, which sits in the middle of the passage between Whidbey Island and the mainland. Technically the eastern end of the bridge connects to Fidalgo Island, but since it is separated from the mainland only by shallow Swinomish Channel, many people are unaware that they are on an island. But an island it is until WA 20 crosses to the mainland over a very high bridge that spans Swinomish Channel.

You come down from that high bridge onto the **Skagit Flats,** which holds some of the Northwest's most productive farmland. Among the crops are tulip, iris, and daffodil bulbs, and each spring the valley floor is composed of bands of solid color as the flowers bloom. Several farms sell tulips retail and will ship them anywhere in the world, as noted in chapter 1.

From the Swinomish Channel bridge eastward you will be on a four-lane highway that rushes you toward the roaring traffic and shopping malls that line I-5. Soon after crossing I-5 you will go through **Sedro Woolley,** a mostly agricultural town where the headquarters for North Cascades National Park are located beside the highway on the eastern edge of town. Here you can stock up on maps, brochures, and other information on traveling through the park. This is also the last place you will have a wide choice

The Skagit River valley, also called Skagit Flats, contains some of the richest soil on earth and virtually anything grows there.

of places to eat until you reach Winthrop, 130 miles and two mountain passes away.

The foothills of the Cascades appear almost immediately after you leave Sedro-Woolley. The highway follows the Skagit River upstream for several miles, and you will always be surrounded by large, dark, and damp trees because the closer you come to the Cascades, the more dense and damp the forest. The Skagit is one of the state's most popular rivers. Steelhead fishermen love to drift it with guides, and naturalists love it because bald eagles migrate down from Canada and Alaska by the hundreds to congregate each fall and feast on salmon.

Just before entering the Cascades, you will go through the town of **Concrete,** so named because it was built around a factory that made—of course—cement. When the factory closed, most citizens expected the town to fade into oblivion, but it has thrived as a recreational and retirement town, and film studios discovered it as a place to shoot stories set in the 1950s because its downtown buildings have hardly changed since that period. One of the films made there was called *This Boy's Life,* based on a true story that happened in Concrete. It starred Robert DeNiro and Leonardo DiCaprio, and told the story of the author Tobias Wolff and his mother living with an abusive man during the 1980s.

After Concrete, you are in the Cascades and the climb begins. The highway still follows the Skagit River, but for most of the year it is hardly more than a shadow of its former self because of the hydroelectric dams built decades ago to supply Seattle with electricity. Sometimes the river is virtually dry, then suddenly a wall of water will come rushing down it as the dam floodgates are opened. Some of the most popular tours in the Cascades are the **Seattle City Light Skagit Tours,** which take much of the day. The Diablo Dam Good Dinner tour costs $40–$55, depending on age, and includes a boat cruise plus an all-you-can-eat chicken dinner after you've toured the dams and power plants and gone for a ride on the Incline Railway lift.

After the Diablo tour, you're back on Highway 20 with lots of climbing to do and sharp curves to navigate. The highway bisects the North Cascades National Park, and the area on both sides of the highway have been designated a National Recreational Area so that some support services for travelers, not permitted within national parks, can be available. The park service also maintains a few campgrounds in the area. But be warned; you can't buy gasoline for almost 75 miles after leaving Marblemount, so check your fuel gauge.

The highway isn't particularly easy to drive at night. Because it is cleared of snow so often, the centerline and edge stripes are scraped off by snowplows, and the paint is hardly visible. During a rainstorm or on a foggy night you must drive at almost a crawl. WA-20 is closed between Marblemount and Mazama during the winter because of the snow that accumulates quickly, deeply and in treacherous drifts. Avalanches are an added danger. The highway usually closes before Christmas and opens in May or June.

You will go over two passes on the way across, 4,855-foot Rainy Pass and 5,477-foot Washington Pass. Just beyond Washington Pass is a turnout above the crooked highway with a view across the jagged peaks. It is one of the most dramatic views in the Cascade Range.

From Washington Pass the highway runs downhill for several miles through open pine forests to the Methow Valley and its Western-themed towns of Winthrop and Mazama. Mazama isn't much for size—it has fewer than half a dozen buildings—but it has some of the nicest family resorts in the area, specializing in outdoor recreation such as cross-country skiing and backpacking.

If you have an extra hour or two, you may want to take a side trip from

Mazama over 6,797-foot Harts Pass to **Slate Peak,** the highest point in Washington to which you can drive the family car. The peak is 7,440 feet high, and the dirt road to it is kept in good condition because it is used by sightseers and hikers on the Pacific Crest Trail, which crosses the road just below the peak. The road ends just below the summit, where an abandoned lookout tower still stands, but it is only about a hundred-yard walk to the tower, where you can see for miles in all directions. The drive itself is one of the most beautiful mountain drives in the state, and is worth a couple of hours off the main highway. Be sure to take your camera.

Winthrop is one of Washington's most popular theme towns. Leavenworth has its Bavarian theme, Lynden is Dutch, Poulsbo is Norwegian, Toppenish is all about cowboys, and Winthrop is the good ole American West. It is rather fitting because the area does have a lot of cattle and hayfields, and it also was the home of Owen Wister, the novelist who wrote America's first Western novel, *The Virginian* (1902), while living here. Winthrop was a ranching town for many years. After the sawmill in Twisp closed, ranching was overtaken by summer residences and tourism. The widow of the sawmill owner offered to match funds if Winthrop adopted the Western theme. They built the false fronts and the tourists came. Now the area has one of the longest cross-country ski trails in the nation and property values continue to rise. The Winthrop tourism folks have an unusual way of describing the drive-through tourists. They are "lickers and clickers" because they stop to buy an ice-cream cone and to take a few pictures before going on their way.

Before you go on your way, take an hour or so to drive up to Sun Mountain Lodge, one of those places that is so beautiful you shouldn't miss it. The complex was built on the top of a mountain so that you have a 360-degree view. It has the largest privately owned hiking and cross-country-skiing trail system in the state, and it has the biggest string of saddle and packhorses. The view from its bar is westward into the North Cascades, and some people who live in the area are fond of heading for the bar in the resort whenever they see a storm brewing in the Cascades. These storms often put on a terrific show as they come down the mountains to the Methow valley.

From Winthrop the highway follows the Methow River south to Twisp. Just south of this small town you have a choice of leaving WA 20 and continuing south on WA 153 to the Columbia River and US 97, or continuing on WA 20 across the state. Here our route, WA 20, swings due east just south of Twisp and enters the first range of rolling, barren hills that lies between the Cascades and the Okanogan highlands. After about thirty miles of ranches and crooked highway and lots of Old West scenery, you arrive in the twin towns of Okanogan and Omak.

While they aren't literally connected—they are about three miles apart—the towns have grown toward each other so much that you can't tell the difference. They are working folks' towns more than tourist destinations, which makes them more interesting because they still have a "real" feel to them. You can find ten-penny nails and irrigation sprinklers in the hardware stores, and the price of a room in a good motel is about half what you will pay in Winthrop or Port Townsend. When restaurant menus offer steak, you will be getting a lot of meat, plus potatoes, salad, and all the coffee you dare drink. One of the most popular places to eat is a small cafe in the Omak stockyards called the Gibson Girls Stockyard Cafe. There's no phone and they don't take reservations; just show up and have meatloaf, chicken-fried steak, or other traditional American dishes.

State 20 joins the busier US 97 in Omak and follows it north about twenty-five miles along the Okanogan River to Tonasket, where WA 20 departs and heads east into the heart of the Okanogan highlands. The highlands include most of the Okanogan and Colville National Forests and the Kettle River Range, a small spur of the Rocky Mountains that dribbled off into Washington from Idaho. This region is noted for cattle, pine timber, gold mines, and the ghost towns that record the history of gold mining. While the highlands aren't as high as the Cascades, still Sherman Creek Pass, at 5,575 feet, is the highest highway pass in the state.

The first town after you leave Tonasket is Wauconda, one of those rare one-building towns that has almost everything you need. It features a gas pump, a post office, a general store, and a restaurant good enough to be written up in newspapers and magazines as a destination. In addition to all of the above, the restaurant also has excellent views across the valley and low mountains.

The next town of more than one building is Republic, another one of those "real" towns that is also interesting. It is a gold-mining town—at this writing, two mines are in operation there—and it also serves ranchers, forest service employees, loggers, and tourists. Its historical museum tells the town's boom-and-bust history. Republic's first gold rush occurred at almost exactly the same time as the Klondike discovery in 1896, and gold has been mined here off and on ever since.

THE TALE OF THREE MOLSONS

Today Molson consists of a few scattered buildings and farm equipment in an open-air museum, a brick school building that is now a museum, and a small cluster of modest homes and a store with gas pumps out front, closed. The first buildings were what is now Old Molson, the schoolhouse was Middle Molson, and the last group of buildings was New Molson.

Few towns or cities in Washington—or anywhere else for that matter—have such an eccentric history as this almost ghost town in the Okanogan Country not far from the Canadian border.

Like most Western ghost towns in the west, Molson began with a gold mine. This one was the Poland China Gold Mine two miles south of the Canadian border in countryside too rugged for a town. Instead, a site four miles west of the mine was selected, a place with treeless rolling hills, a seasonal stream and a supply of trees for building material and firewood within walking distance. Here two men pooled their talents and resources to build the town: John Molson of the Canadian brewing family, a heavy investor in the mine, and George Meacham, a promoter.

The ghost town of Old Molson is straight ahead.

In 1900 Molson put up $75,000 in the new town, which bore his name. He built a drugstore, a newspaper, and the town's showpiece, the three-story Tonasket Hotel. It had a glass front, a wraparound second-story balustrade and more than 60 full-height windows.

The town had hardly been built before its population reached three hundred. Sadly, at the same time, the Poland China mine began coughing up rocks and dirt, but no precious metals. People began moving away, and those who stayed went into farming and livestock. Then homesteaders began arriving in the area, and in 1904 a store and grain warehouse was built, along with a mercantile store. A small railroad came through town, and soon Molson had eight saloons. A deputy sheriff was sent up from the county seat at Okanogan to keep peace in the small but booming town.

Then along came a man named J.H. McDonald, surely one of the most insensitive and greedy men in Washington history. McDonald filed for a home-stead of 160 acres. The only thing wrong with his filing was that it included near-ly the entire city of Molson, including the Hotel Tonasket. Nobody had bothered to file for the land on which Molson stood. McDonald had them cold. Nobody could do anything about it.

McDonald further endeared himself by posting notices to the squatters. Thus the storekeepers had to move half a mile north, where they built a new town. By 1906, Old Molson and New Molson were about the same size, and the hatred between the two towns was deep and permanent. Residents of the two towns fought over every imagined slight and threat.

McDonald kept up his campaign of diplomacy by fencing the entire town of Old Molson, and in the same year he accomplished that, 1908, a man named Work built a bank and placed it in Old Molson. However, McDonald wouldn't permit him to obtain legal ownership of land on which to put his bank, so Work put the bank on skids and moved it from place to place each day—or night—and

The three Molsons are spread out across the top of the photo, and the Inn at Molson B&B is in the foreground.

his customers never knew from one day to the next where they would find the bank. Fortunately, Old Molson was quite small, so it was usually a matter of walking down the main street and looking north and south for it, or listening for the telltale grinding of the skids on the roadrock. Finally Work was able to find a permanent resting place and when he had it firmly anchored, he had a grand-opening party, which of course soon became a free-for-all street fight.

This rancor continued year after year, and the only truce the two towns recognized was the matter of a school. Since neither town had enough children to support their own school, they managed to agree on this and built a brick school roughly halfway between the two towns. It was a rather grand school for the size of the towns and the era, and had a large auditorium on the main floor, steam heat, two floors of classrooms, and an indoor gymnasium. The school generated a small building boom as people who hated the continual bickering looked for a middle ground. A theater was built there, and so were a mercantile store, a pool hall and a barbershop.

The fighting continued, though, and each town tried to out-do the other. When one got a theater, the other built one. The same happened with nice homes, and finally with auto dealerships. When one dealer sold Oaklands, another sprang up in the other town and sold Maxwells.

Old Molson had kept the post office, which rankled New Molsonites, and they tried several legal avenues to get their own post office. Nothing worked, so one day when the postmaster was at lunch, New Molsonites stole the whole post office and moved it.

The fighting continued into the 1920s, when Molson began receding further and further from a town status toward ghost-town status. By the 1950s, very few citizens were left, and by the 1960s Molson—actually all three—were relegated to the ghost town category.

The town had its share of ups and downs and promoters who came and went. Promoters in the nineteenth century were perhaps the most positive people who ever lived, and those in Republic talked endlessly of how the town would soon be a major metropolis. They also talked about a railroad that was going to come to town anytime. They talked about this one so much that the (imaginary) railroad became known as the Hot Air Line. To the skeptics' chagrin, in 1902 a line was built south from Grand Forks, just across the border in British Columbia, and was soon taken over by the Great Northern line. But that was then. Now the railroad is a memory.

The Stonerose fossil bed is a very short walk from the **Stonerose Interpretive Center** at 15-1 N. Kean St. The bed itself is at the edge of town on private land but permission to dig is given by the volunteer staff in the museum. Most of the fossils are of leaves, including those of a rose—the so-called stone rose—which has been extinct for nobody knows how long.

From Republic the highway climbs through the beautiful pine forests and open meadows, clears 5,575-foot Sherman Pass, and coasts down to Roosevelt Lake of the Columbia River at **Kettle Falls.** This town is distinguished by a sign on the outskirts proclaiming its population, and below that is a smaller sign, in bold letters and suitably illustrated, proclaiming that it also has one grouch. A contest is held each year to appoint the year's grouch. Before the Columbia River dams, Kettle Falls actually was a waterfall. Like so many interesting features along the river, the backwaters of Roosevelt Lake covered the falls.

A major north–south route, US 395, is crossed at Kettle Falls, but WA 20 continues its eastward run, this time through the worn-down Selkirk Mountains to the tiny town of Tiger on the Pend Oreille River. This is a region of small valleys, pine-covered hillsides, and inexpensive resorts on small lakes that cater to families. You won't find many of these resorts listed in the expensive magazines because they are usually basic and reasonably priced; cabins with furniture but no bedding, wood stoves, and community showers are common. Fishing for trout and bass is popular, as is hunting for deer, elk, and black bear. You may see an occasional moose in these forests, and grizzly bears aren't common but they do occasionally wander through. Wolves and coyotes visit, and infrequently the woodland caribou herd from Idaho and southern British Columbia comes through.

The highway follows the banks of the slow, stately Pend Oreille River south to Newport on the Idaho state line, where WA 20 disappears into the transcontinental US 2.

IN THE AREA

Port Townsend

Accommodations

Ann Starrett Mansion, 744 Clay St., Port Townsend. Call 360-385-3205. The mansion is one of Port Townsend's most elaborate Victorians. With the old carriage house added to the mix, it has a wide variety of rooms of several shapes and sizes. Web site: www.starrettmansion.com

Baker House B&B. 905 Franklin St. Call 360-385-6673 or 800-240-0725. This remodeled Victorian home offers some of the best views in town, taking in Puget Sound, the town's waterfront, and the mountains. There are four guest rooms. Email: hnjherrington@olympus.net

Bishop Victorian Hotel, 714 Washington St. Call 360-385-6122 or 800-824-4738. A block off the main drag and the waterfront, this hotel features 16 suites, some with soaking tubs, fireplaces, and kitchenettes. Web site: www.bishopvictorian.com

Captain Whidbey Inn, 2072 Captain Whidbey Rd., Coupeville. Call 360-678-4097 or 800-366-4097. Rooms in the main building are what brochure writers love to call "cozy," which means they are small and their uneven, tilting floors squeak. That's just fine with the many people who love this place for its charming oldness; there are also cottages for rent.

Commander's Beach House, 400 Hudson St. Call 360-385-1778. This B&B is at the northern edge of town on the beach, yet only a short stroll to the center of town. Each of its three rooms has a view of the Puget Sound. Web site: www.commandersbeachhouse.com

Old Consulate Inn, 313 Walker St. Call 360-385-6753. So named because it housed the German consulate around the turn of the 20th century, the Old Consulate has eight rooms, all with private bath. Breakfast is known as the "banquet breakfast" thanks to its generous three-course, seven-dish presentation. Web site: www.oldconsulateinn.com

Palace Hotel & Captain Tibbals, 1004 Water St. Call 360-385-0773. This hotel has 14-foot ceilings and 10-foot arched windows. The 17 rooms range from Continental style to suites, some with views of Puget Sound. Web site: www.palacehotelpt.com

Attractions and Recreation

Seattle City Light Skagit Tours. Call 206-684-3030. E-mail: Skagit-Tours.Reservations@seattle.gov

Dining

Fountain Café, 920 Washington St. Call 360-385-1364. Daily seafood specials are accompanied by Northwest beer and wine, and followed by homemade desserts.

Landfall, 412 Water St. Call 360-385-5814. This self-proclaimed seafood dive serves only breakfast and lunch. The menu is expansive and imaginative.

Local Goods, Fort Worden Commons. Call 360-344-4440. Several soup and sandwich options are offered here, plus assorted coffee and espresso drinks.

Salal Café, 634 Water Street. Call 360-385-6532. Breakfast is a specialty here and is served all day, in addition to lunch.

Upstage Restaurant & Theater, 923 Washington St. Call 360-385-2216. Some of the top blues and jazz artists in the country perform at the Upstage, and the food is also good. Pizzas, seafood, and salads are some of the popular choices.

Winthrop Area

Accommodations

Chewuch Inn & Cabins, 223 White Ave., Winthrop. Call 509-996-3107 or 800-747-3107. This 17-room inn is a short walk along the Methow River from the shops of downtown Winthrop. Some rooms have king-size beds, fireplaces, and soaking tubs. A full breakfast is included. Web site: www.chewuchinn.com

Freestone Inn & Cabins, 31 Early Winters Dr. #11, Mazama. Call 509-996-3906 or 800-639-3809. This complex includes 15 cabins and three lodges on Early Winters Creek, all completely equipped for preparing your own meals. Guests can make use of the resort's own helicopter pad. Web site: www.freestoneinn.com

Sojourns Guesthouse, Twisp. Call 509-997-0576. This unusual guest house guarantees privacy for each couple, small group, or family who rents it. With up to three bedrooms per party, it is something like a large apartment. A three-course breakfast is included. Web site: www.sojourns guesthouse.com

Sun Mountain Lodge, Patterson Lake Rd., Winthrop. Call 509-996-2211 or 800-572-0493. Perched atop Sun Mountain, with commanding views north into the Pasayten Wilderness and west across the Cascade Mountains into North Cascades National Park, the Sun Mountain Lodge is one of the most spectacular resorts in Washington. The property has several miles of cross-country skiing trails, and offers horseback riding, biking, tennis, and just plain strolling in an area remote enough to make you believe you're alone in the world. The restaurants are excellent, and the bar has great views across the mountains. Web site: www.sunmountain lodge.com

Attractions and Recreation

Stonerose Interpretive Center at 15-1 N. Kean St., Republic. Call 509-775-2295.

Dining

Boulder Creek Deli, 100 Bridge St., Winthrop. Call 509-996-2192. The Boulder Creek menu is basically ten different sandwiches featuring roast beef and turkey. Soups, salads, and calzones are also on offer. If you eat inside, you can enjoy the deli's famous "heiferglyphics" mural or dancing cows.

Heenan's Burnt Finger Bar-B-Q & Steak House, 716 Highway 20 South, Winthrop. Call 509-996-8221. Grilled steaks and burgers are accompanied by live cowboy music on weekends, with a dance floor to boot.

Twisp River Pub, 201 N. Highway 20, Twisp. Call 509-997-6822. overlooking the Methow River from a deck, this casual place serves freshly brewed beers and what the owner calls "real food." Web site: www.methow brewing.com

Other Contacts

Central Whidbey Chamber of Commerce & Visitor Information Center, 23 NW Front St. (in Mariners Court Bldg.), Coupeville. Call 1-888-747-7777.

Concrete Chamber of Commerce, Main St., Concrete. Call 360-853-7621.

Kettle Falls Chamber of Commerce, 265 W. 3rd Ave., Kettle Falls. Call 509-738-2300.

Mount Vernon Chamber of Commerce, 105 E. Kincaid St., Mount Vernon. Call 360-428-8547.

North Cascades National Park Service Complex, 810 State Route 20 (at Highway 9 north), Sedro-Woolley. Call 360-854-7200.

Okanogan Chamber of Commerce, 211 Queen St., Okanogan. Call 509-422-2383.

Omak Chamber of Commerce, 401 Omak Ave., Omak. Call 509-826-1880.

Port Townsend Chamber of Commerce, 440 12th St., Port Townsend. Call 360-385-2722.

Republic Chamber of Commerce, 65 N. Clark Ave., Republic. Call 509-775-2704.

Washington State Ferries. Call 1-888-808-7977 or 206-464- 6400, or 511 between 7 and 5:45. Web site: https://business.wsdot.wa.gov/ferries/reservations.

Winthrop Chamber of Commerce, 202 Riverside Ave., Winthrop. Call 509-996-2125 or 1-888-463-8469.

Not much is left of the ghost town of Nighthawk, in part because people have moved back in, rendering the ghost-town designation suspect.

Okanogan Loop

Estimated length: 116 miles
Estimated time: 4–6 hours

Getting there: From Omak go west on West Cherry Street, then north on Conconully Road. From Conconully take Lake Street northeast, which becomes Similkameen Road. Continue north through Loomis to Nighthawk and turn east on Loomis-Oroville Road to Oroville and WA 97. Continue across WA 97 and turn left on Cherry Street, which becomes Chesaw Road. After 8 miles, turn left on Molson Road. Take Chesaw Road on the southern edge of Molson and follow it to Chesaw and on to Wauconda, where you will rejoin WA 20.

Highlights: You'll see some of the Okanogan Highlands' most beautiful scenery on this long loop. Conconully is a favorite camping and picnic place for locals, and the Similkameen Valley has become almost entirely orchards in the past several years.

The three-Molson story is one of Washington's strangest, and Chesaw is one of the state's most remote towns.

Several years ago, on the spur of the moment, two friends and I had no plans for the Fourth of July so we picked a town at random to visit for the celebration. It was Conconully. None of us had been there and the other two hadn't even heard of the town. We drove across the Cascades and arrived in Conconully an hour or so before the fireworks began.

Conconully is a very small town, no more than two hundred residents, but here you will find the beautiful man-made **Conconully Lake,** with Conconully State Park, on the edge of town. The town consists of the tavern we ate in, a grocery store, and a few other businesses.

We ate a hamburger in the tavern while watching the drama of the day-to-day life of the locals. This included a young man sitting at the bar slowly sipping beer, when a young woman came in and sat beside him. His attitude improved considerably during their chat. She excused herself to go to the restroom, and when she stood he saw her body for the first time: she was well along in a pregnancy and he looked stricken. We watched as she returned and as she let him twist in the breeze until at last she told him she was married and the baby was definitely not his. We expected him to faint with relief, but he managed to stay on the barstool until she left.

After this bit of drama, we drove about midway up Conconully Lake to watch the fireworks. We later agreed that it was one of the nicest Fourth of July celebrations any of us had ever had, even though not much happened. We had talked to a lot of people, including a part-time real estate agent who tried to sell us some property on the lake. I should have bought some.

This loop trip that includes Conconully begins in downtown Omak. You'd best ask directions to Conconully in case West Cherry Street is marked no better now than it was then, which was not at all. Once you find West Cherry, stay on it until it intersects with Conconully Road. It is a pretty drive out across the rolling hills that surround valleys where hay and fruit are grown. On our weekend the fields were littered with bales of hay that would soon be loaded onto long trucks for me to follow slowly, very slowly, over the Cascades to the horsey set along Puget Sound. Most of the hilltops have a fringe of timber, although some are completely bald.

A gravel road leads from Conconully north along the Similkameen Creek and valley, and passes a scattering of small lakes before arriving at Loomis. Loomis and Nighthawk are two towns with more than one life each. They were built by gold miners, then abandoned as ghost towns, then recently revived as the area became populated and orchards were planted in the valley. Now nearly every acre that can be cultivated is planted with fruit trees and irrigated from the creek and Palmer Lake, created by a dam near Nighthawk.

ROUGH TIME IN RUBY

Like many towns in the Okanogan, Ruby isn't what it used to be because it was built for a silver discovery, and didn't survive when the rush faded. While it last-ed, it was a colorful place, and proved that the Wild West didn't end at the Rockies.

In 1879, the whole area north from Lake Chelan to the Canadian border was an Indian reservation for the Columbia-Wenatchee Indians, but that was changed in 1886 after the settlers and miners complained bitterly that the Indi-ans had the best land in the region. At that time the reservation was reduced to the present Colville Indian Reservation boundaries.

When the reservation lands were reduced, people rushed out to stake claims. One, a deputy sheriff named E.J. Dorian, told of going out to stake his claim next to a county commissioner. The only trouble was that they were there before the reservation was formally reduced, so they did what claim-stakers have always done: they "squatted," meaning they posted and hoped it would last until the official date of May 1.

"The day the reservation opened," he said, "both the county commissioner and I were in Colville on county business. We rode night and day to get back to out places in time to protect them, and even changed horses. But the trip lasted four days and on our arrival we found others had gotten there first."

Two years later Guy Waring, a pioneer in the area and excellent writer, told of an incident at one of the sporting houses.

"On this particular afternoon the town was in the heat of excitement over the latest of its many notorious murders which, as I soon learned, had occurred early that same morning. It seems that one of Ruby's more lecherous citizens had attempted shortly before dawn to gain admittance to the town's chief bawdy house in a state of complete intoxication. When the mistress of the house, great-ly annoyed at being diverted from her business at such an hour, refused to per-mit him to enter, the gentleman, according to the report I gathered, took a swing at her.

"Thereupon the mistress, not to miss having the last word on the doorstep of her own establishment, returned to her room and shot the gentleman through the heart, killing him instantly. His body had been found crumpled upon the steps outside the house, and by the time the sheriff could be persuaded to inquire at the establishment for details of the 'accident' the mistress had found time to board the stage for Spokane Falls, knowing, of course, that a few days later the whole affair would be forgotten in the interest of some new scandal in the town, and she could return unmolested by the law to her former mode of living.

"As I listened to a group of citizens expound the merits of the case, I gained a still better idea of the level of morality one could expect to find in Ruby . . . I went to the county auditor's office, where I was forced to listen to a further version of the murder by an official who, as he had casually explained, had been inside the brothel at the time of the shooting and stumbled over the dead body on his way out in the morning."

Just north of Nighthawk is the Canadian border with a customs station that is open only part of the time. It is rumored to be one of the loneliest customs posts along the U.S.–Canadian border. One friend entered the United States from Canada at this point and he said the border patrolman was so lonely he wanted a conversation, while my friend was in a hurry.

The main route turns east at Nighthawk and follows the river valley down into **Oroville,** only a couple of miles from the Canadian border. Since gasoline is cheaper in the U.S., several large service stations have been built in Oroville for Canadian visitors. The town also has a scattering of antiques shops and restaurants. Oroville is at the southern tip of Lake Osoyoos, which straddles the international border and is a popular camping and picnic area. Washington has established a state park on its side and Canada has resorts and summer homes on its part of the lake. You'll note on maps that in the U.S. the region is spelled *Okanogan.* Across the border it is spelled *Okanagan.*

From here you can continue east and visit the three Molsons, described in chapter 4, and rejoin WA 20 at Wauconda.

IN THE AREA

Accommodations

The Inn at Molson, 31 Mary Ann Creek Rd., Oroville. Call 509-485-2018. The inn has three bedrooms appointed with antiques and handmade items. Breakfast is included, and dinner, priced between $15 and $35 per person, is available by reservation.

Other Contacts

Conconully Chamber of Commerce, 219 N. Main St., Riverside. Call 826-0813.

Okanogan Chamber of Commerce, 211 Queen St., Okanogan. Call 422-0441.

Tonasket Chamber of Commerce, 7 N. Western Ave., Tonasket. Call 486-2931.

All grain elevators are tall, but each has its own distinctive appearance.

6

Wandering through the Palouse Country

Estimated length: 90 miles
Estimated time: Half a day

Getting there: In general, this route follows WA 27 between Pullman and Opportunity in the Spokane Valley. In the Palouse it is best to wander at will, taking any road that is paved, to enjoy this unusual area. The only true must-see is Steptoe Butte, with the small and modest state park at its base and the fantastic view from the summit. Otherwise, amble, stop in small towns for a meal or coffee and enjoy the ambience of small-town life in a beautiful landscape.

Highlights: This ramble will show you the beautiful rolling hills of the Palouse, some of the best wheat-growing land in the world. You will also visit small and unpretentious towns, seeing the landscape laid out before you from the top of a unique mountain named Steptoe Butte.

Although it describes a geographic area as well as an abbreviation for the popular saddle horse called Appaloosa, the origins of the word *Palouse* are something of a mystery. Nobody knows exactly what it meant in the language of the Native Americans, from whom whites borrowed the word. They called themselves Palouse, or something similar, but they didn't know why, nor did they know what the word meant. Today the name means some of the most productive farming land in the world, and to those of us who like open landscapes, it means one of the most beautiful parts of Washington.

The Palouse country has no distinct boundaries, but in general it runs north from the Snake River to the Spokane River valley, west into the channeled scablands, which are bordered (more or less) on the west by I-90, and the eastern boundary is where the timber begins in Idaho. The landscape is notable for its deep soil, which is loess, meaning it has been blown in by the wind that comes out of the southwest every day, steady and dependable as a river. The soil is more than 100 feet deep in some places.

Most of the Palouse is low but steep, rolling hills with an elevation that ranges from about 1,200 feet to a little more than 2,000 feet. This altitude gain is crucial to the Palouse because the elevation catches the rainfall that skips over the area from the Cascade Range to the Palouse, which includes the Columbia Basin and the dryland wheat-farming area west of the channeled scablands. This elevation gain is impossible to detect as you drive east, but it shows up dramatically in the wheat production figures. The Palouse gets thirty bushels or more per acre than wheat farms only a short distance west. As with all agriculture, the amount of rainfall makes the difference. A great advantage the Palouse farmers have over their Great Plains counterparts is the almost total absence of crop loss to weather. A few years ago the head of the cooperative extension service in Pullman told me that the Palouse farmers had never had a crop failure. "Never!" he emphasized.

When the first mobile combines were built to thresh wheat, the steep hills of the Palouse created major problems. The body of the combine, called the separator because it is where the grain is separated from the stalks and chaff, must be kept level in order to work properly. The earliest mobile combines' separators were kept level by turning large wheels on ratchets to raise and lower each side. In the Palouse with its uneven terrain and steep hills known as "side hills," this meant a lot of work. Then when the first self-propelled combines, operated by only one person, were developed, they were good only on flatland, such as the Great Plains.

Enter a man from the Palouse named Hansen. Some of his neighbors called him "Haywire" Hansen because he was always building things, inventing easier ways to do things. It wasn't long before Hansen had a solution to the combine-leveling problem: He invented a motorized ratchet system that kicked on and off by a mercury switch. When the combine tilted, the mercury slid down to trip the switch, which started a motor or hydraulic pump that raised or lowered one side of the combine until it was level. Then the mercury returned to the middle of the switch, much like the bubble in a leveling device, breaking electrical contact to shut off the level. For wheat farmers, this invention was almost as important as the internal combustion engine.

One of the best times to take a trip through these steep Palouse Hills is in the spring when everything is green, and the best time of day is early or late when the shadows sharply define the landscape. My favorite drive is on US 27, which begins in Pullman and ends in the Spokane River valley at Opportunity. It is a slow and crooked highway lined with mailboxes and farmhouses, and you'll share it with tractors pulling various farm equipment from field to field and farmers who often drive slowly so they can look at their crops and check fences.

A short distance out of Pullman you'll come to the turn to Kamiak Butte State Park, featuring a 3,360-foot peak that stands high above the rolling hills. It was named for a Yakima chief named Kamiakin, a notable warrior who defeated the U.S. Army from time to time.

The first town out of Pullman is Palouse, on the banks of the river of the same name. The town has lots of brick buildings, and although the great old hardware store finally closed and sold off its fixtures to a local collector, most of Palouse's small-town charm remains. Palouse is close enough to the Western Washington University crowd at Pullman and the gentry of Spokane to have a deli with specialty coffee.

As you drive along this road, and several other more modest two-lane roads, you'll notice that, although the road may have been perfectly straight as it went across the farmlands, just before it enters a town it makes one, sometimes two, sudden sharp turns. This was planned. It was an effort by highway engineers to force drivers to slow down before entering towns.

Just north of Palouse, in Garfield, is a county road leading off to the west, marked ELBERTON. It is worth an hour's delay to drive over to visit the remnants of this once-thriving town. It can't accurately be called a ghost town because people still live there, but most of the businesses and churches were moved elsewhere after Elberton was disincorporated in 1966. It has the odd distinction of being the only town in Washington that closed shop, in a manner of speaking. An effort was made in the 1970s to turn the remnants of the town into a working museum, with the post office and general store still functioning. But funds weren't forthcoming and the town, once an important milling center, returned to its status of being

Steptoe Butte is one of the most familiar landmarks in the Palouse.

mostly a memory. Still, Elberton was beautifully sited on the Palouse River, with ancient trees lining the street and riverbank.

Another good side trip is from Oakesdale on WA 27 to **Steptoe Butte State Park.** As parks go, this one is small—just a picnic table or two at the foot of the peak—but the peak itself is much more impressive. It rises 3,600 feet above the Palouse hills and its summit is reached by a road that corkscrews around and around until it reaches the top. Once there you will have wonderful views of the Palouse hills, especially early in the morning and late in the evening; just. But it is best to keep your back to the actual summit because it bristles with radio and television transmission towers.

Steptoe was named for Colonel Edward J. Steptoe, who in 1858 was soundly defeated by Native Americans.

Steptoe Butte was later purchased by one of those extremely self-confident, slightly eccentric Englishmen who appeared frequently on the frontier. James Davis and his brother came to America in 1840, but, unlike most immigrants, they did not travel in steerage. Davis had in his "luggage" a fine team of horses, an elegant surrey, a pair of hunting hounds, and some expensive hunting rifles.

THE STEPTOE DEFEAT

In 1858, eighteen years before the Custer disaster at Little Big Horn, Washington Territory was almost the scene of an equally resounding victory by the Indians against the encroaching whites. On this occasion, the man in charge of the ill-fated Army expedition was Colonel Edward Steptoe. He left his name on the battlefield, on a small town that appeared later, and on a pyramid-shaped peak.

Steptoe was the commanding officer of Fort Walla Walla, but his sympathies were with the Indians whom the territorial governor, Isaac Stevens, had been badgering, bullying, and virtually forcing to sign treaties that the Indians did not really understand. Like most Army career officers, Steptoe knew the Indians were being treated unfairly, yet he was charged with the safety of civilians who were coming into Washington Territory, particularly into what is now Idaho, in increasing numbers to seek gold.

Col. Steptoe was lucky when he was commander of a fiasco: very few people ever heard about it.

During the two years of Stevens's treaty efforts, a Yakima chief, Kamiakin, had been making the rounds among all Indians from the Snake River north spreading the message that the Indians should evict the white settlers before they became too numerous. Adding to the Indians' resentment was the construction of a road between Fort Walla Walla and Fort Benton, the head of navigation on the Missouri River over in Montana. Although the road, named the Mullan Road in honor of the Army captain in charge of construction, never amounted to much, it still represented an intrusion along a 1,000-mile route into the Indians' territory. More and more rumors of an impending Indian uprising, and reports of a few killings, filtered back to Fort Walla Walla and forced Steptoe to take action. Much of the unrest was reported in the area of present-day Colville, and the Palouse Indians, who were near enough to Fort Walla Walla for Steptoe to know they weren't docile, had been helping Kamiakin to spread the uprising fever.

In May 1858, Steptoe decided to make an expedition into the Spokane Indians' territory to discuss treaties that had been signed by the Indians and Stevens but were not yet ratified by the Senate. Steptoe organized a troop of 152 enlisted men, six officers, and a few Nez Perce scouts. All were mounted, and an additional one hundred packhorses were in the train.

It was the contents of the packs carried by the horses that caused Steptoe's serious troubles. The chief packer, who later admitted his mistake, loaded the packs with food and camping equipment but no ammunition. The only ammunition was on the men's belts. Steptoe was not aware of this until the fighting began, and he was ultimately blamed for not knowing the contents of his field equipment.

He thought it would be a leisurely trek. Only the Palouse Indians were unfriendly, and Steptoe wanted to meet with them early in the trip to apprehend the murderers of two miners. But the Palouse withdrew from the Snake River and preceded Steptoe's troops north, joining with the Spokane and Coeur d'Alene tribes to build their forces. Kamiakin was there, organizing the tribes into a war machine.

They met on May 15, 1858, when Steptoe camped on Pine Creek near present-day Rosalia. The Indians set up an ambush in a gulch and waited for the troops to enter it. Scouts saw them and Steptoe detoured around the gulch, and camped that night at a small lake. The Indians later told historians the only thing that saved him from being attacked that day was the fact that it was Sunday, which reflected some of the religious teachings the Indians had been exposed to in missions in the area.

Only after a battle seemed certain did Steptoe discover the ammunition situation, and he ordered a retreat for the following morning. A scout was sent ahead to get reinforcements from Fort Walla Walla to meet Steptoe's forces at the Snake River crossing. Steptoe believed he could outrun the Indians to the river, but the crossing itself was an excellent place for ambushes.

The soldiers had traveled only about five miles when the Indians attacked. A chief was called into a meeting by the missionary, Father Joset, who had dashed over from the Cataldo Mission in Idaho. The chief, called Vincent, was insulted and slapped by a Nez Perce scout. The battle began.

The soldiers had no water, precious little ammunition, and their guns weren't as modern as those the Indians had purchased from the Hudson's Bay Company in Canada. Nor were they carrying their cutlasses, and there was much hand-to-hand combat. The running battle continued on and off all day and until nightfall, when it was the Indians' turn to make a mistake. They believed the soldiers would be easy prey the following day, and backed off to celebrate the day's fighting and to divide the spoils from the packhorses they had managed to capture.

During the night Steptoe organized his escape. He sent scouts south to see if they could get through the Indians' lines, and the scouts returned without seeing any of the hostile Indians. The soldiers piled their baggage in plain sight on the hill where they had stopped, buried their dead along with the few virtually useless field howitzers, and led horses back and forth over the fresh earth to disguise the graves. They converted some of the packhorses into mounts to replace the 30-odd that had been shot out from under the troopers. They put blankets over all white horses and did what they could to pad the metal parts of harnesses and saddles that might clink and rattle. They accomplished all this within two hours after the fighting ceased, and then they divided into two groups and began sneaking off into the night.

Steptoe led the hungry, thirsty, and tired troops south to the Palouse River, where they took a brief rest and had their first drinking water in two days. They lashed the wounded into their saddles, and eventually had to abandon two men while they were still alive because the men preferred being left behind to the agony of riding. Both had worked loose from the lashings and fallen from their horses.

After a ride of 25 hours with virtually no rest, the weary troops arrived at the Snake River early in the morning and managed to cross it without loss of men or horses, aided by a group of Nez Perce camped nearby. Late that morning the reinforcements arrived from Fort Walla Walla, indicating that the scout sent ahead had made the harrowing trip of more than 100 miles in less than 36 hours, certainly one of the hardest rides in Washington's history.

Colonel Steptoe was ruined by the incident, despite his brilliant retreat. The matter of the overlooked ammunition was his downfall. He died in disgrace (at least in his own mind) in 1865.

The end of this Indian uprising came shortly after Steptoe's defeat. Colonel George Wright was sent out to put an end to the hostilities, and he pursued his mission with exceptional vigor. He followed the scorched-earth policy of killing as many Indians as he could find, destroying their villages and supplies, and hanging their chiefs. Moreover, he came to enjoy it. Wright's most effective act probably was one that he did not completely appreciate himself until well afterward. When his troops managed to capture some seven hundred horses, Colonel Wright ordered the animals all shot. The Indians were demoralized by this cold-blooded destruction of the universal sign of wealth, and it was an act totally foreign to their way of thinking. Horses were to be stolen, but never killed.

In Wright's report, he wrote: "The chastisement which these Indians have received has been severe but well merited, and absolutely necessary to impress them with our power. For the last 80 miles our route has been marked by slaughter and devastation; 900 horses and a large number of cattle have been killed or appropriated to our own use; many houses, with large quantities of wheat and oats, also many caches of vegetables, kamas [camas], and dried berries, have been destroyed. A blow has been struck which they will never forget."

The plain-front hotel stood many years on top of Steptoe Butte, but eventually burned and was not replaced.

This may have been the most destructive such raid in the history of American Indian warfare, but since the area was so remote from the rest of the nation at that time, little notice was taken of the expeditions then, or since.

SPOKANE GARRY

Few Washington pioneers had more strength of character or were more dignified the Spokane Indian chief named Spokane Garry. Few heads of state in history have been treated with more contempt by an enemy than the whites heaped upon his life during his old age. He was born the eldest son of a chief named Illim-Spokanee of the Sin-ho-man-naish, or salmon-trout people, a band that later became known as the Middle Spokanes. Spokane meant, more or less, children of the sun, and these bands of Indians apparently got the name because when they fished at Spokane Falls, they often stood in a rainbow or halo caused by the sunlight hitting the mist that flew up from the falls. Another version is that the name came from Illim-Spokanee (or Illum-Spokane, as it was sometimes spelled).

Spokane Garry's life was changed forever when he was selected by the Hudson's Bay superintendent, Sir George Simpson, to take part in an experiment. Simpson seemed to think that the best thing the whites could do for all concerned was to teach Indian children the white man's ways so they could go among their people and cause or help them to adapt to the white man's world. Simpson asked the local chief factor, Alexander Ross, to "pick for me a promising boy of the Middle Spokanes and another of the Kootenais to be sent to the Protestant mission school conducted at Red River Settlement."

Ross went to Illim-Spokanee and the Indians held several meetings among themselves before they decided to send the future chief, which was exactly what Simpson would have wanted. It was here that his name, Garry, was acquired in honor of a Hudson's Bay official, and he was accompanied by a boy who became known as Kootenai Pelly, named for the same man whose name was also placed on a river in the Yukon. Unfortunately, the other boy died at school, but Garry stayed five years to learn English and French. He also became a convert to Christianity of the Protestant variety.

On his return, he became chief of both the Upper and Middle Spokanes, was given two wives, and started a school where he taught religion and agriculture. He was also the man to whom whites turned when they wanted to negotiate with the local Indians, a position that often placed him in a precarious position. He obviously could not keep both groups happy, and he was frequently criticized by both.

Some whites were more difficult than others, and among the hardest to please were the missionaries, particularly Cushing Eells and Elkanah Walker, who, according to the historian Lucile F. Fargo, "were not particularly gifted in the art of sympathetic understanding." The Catholic and Protestant missionaries caused Garry much grief, so much that when Sir George Simpson visited him in 1841, he found Garry filthy and unkept, and completely disgusted with life in general. But he recovered soon and went back to work trying to keep peace between the whites and Indians, the Catholics and Protestants, the British and the Americans. His recovery was so complete that by the time Territorial Governor Isaac Ingalls Stevens arrived in 1853 en route to Olympia, Garry was very much in command of the Spokane Falls area, and was running a flour mill on the Little Spokane River and was the neatest Indian Stevens had laid his eyes on during his travels across the West.

But trouble was slowly brewing. More and more whites were arriving, and as their numbers increased, the quality of the Indians' lives decreased. Stevens wouldn't give each tribe of interior Indians their tribal lands, trying instead to lump several tribes together. Since the Indians had always had tribal rivalries that ranged from outright warfare to simple disagreements, they weren't at all interested in this.

When Stevens had his Walla Walla meeting, Spokane Garry attended so he could see what to expect when Stevens moved north to negotiate with his and other tribes. The chief didn't like what he saw, and when the council was finally held, he spoke with eloquence. He also had the advantage of those early years in the white's educational system, and more than perhaps any other Indian of his generation in that area, he knew both sides of the issue. The future was all too obvious: The Indians had lost. But he would still try to reason.

"When you look at the red men, you think you have more heart, more sense, than these poor Indians. I think that the difference between us and you Americans is in the clothing; the blood and the body are the same. Do you think that because your mother was white and theirs dark, that you are higher or better?

"We are dark, yet if we cut ourselves the blood is red, so with the whites it is the same, though their skin is white. I do not think we are poor because we belong to another nation.

"If you take the Indians for men, treat them so now.

"If you talk to the Indians to make peace, the Indian will do the same to you.

"You see, now, the Indians are proud. On account of one of your remarks, some of your people have already fallen to the ground.

"The Indians are not satisfied with the land you gave them. If those Indians had marked out their own reservations, the trouble would not have happened. If you could get their reservations made a little larger they would be pleased. If I had the business to do, I could fix it by giving them a little more land."

Although things didn't end well for Garry's people, it wasn't necessarily Stevens' fault. The diminutive governor liked Garry and tried to keep the Spokanes away from the Indian Wars that swept across the state.

When Col. Steptoe began his ill-fated march north in May, 1858, Garry and other chiefs rode out to meet him to express their desire for peace. Col. Steptoe believed them and told Garry that his orders were to march on north into the Colville area, where the appeal for help had come from. But he didn't make it. He was attacked south of the Spokane area. While his losing battle did not involve the Spokanes, that made no difference. When Col. George Wright made his scorched-earth revenge mission in September of the same year, he made no distinction between "good" and "bad" Indians; any Indians within sight were shot in the battle some 15 miles south of Spokane. It lasted about four hours and three of Garry's bothers and a brother-in-law were killed.

Grief-stricken, Garry met with Col. Wright and told him his people should not be punished for the mistakes of a few. Wright was not impressed. He told Garry to go back and tell all Indians—men, women, and children—to come in and lay down their arms.

When Garry left his camp, Wright ordered his men to march again. The first chief who surrendered to Wright was hung. Then they rounded up between more than eight hundred head of horses and slaughtered them. Then they burned all buildings that had grain stored in them.

This completely demoralized the Indians. Killing the horses was the equivalent of destroying all the banks in Switzerland. Garry and other chiefs met Wright on Latah Creek and signed the so-called peace treaty offered them on September 23, 1858. The name of Latah Creek was soon changed to Hangman Creek because ten Indians were hanged in pine trees along the creek.

Spokane Garry was a changed man after that. Although he was still respected by most, and still called upon for arbitration and as a spokesman, his way of life reflected that of his race in general; it was a series of humiliations. Under terms of the treaty he had signed, Indians had the same rights to their land as the whites who took land under the homestead laws. He had a piece of land that he "proved up" with crops, a fence and buildings, but when he went to a fishing camp on the Spokane River with his family, whites came in and took over his home. Since he was Indian, the courts wouldn't help him.

Things got worse. He was old and the pension promised him by the white government never came. His wife died, and he and his daughter Nelly were left in a teepee on Hangman Creek, where his cattle were stolen, and children rolled stones down the hill onto his teepee. His few remaining head cattle were stolen, and he had to rely on gifts of food and clothing from the few other Indians who could help him, and precious few sympathetic whites.

Death finally came to him in his teepee in 1892. He was buried in a white man's cemetery.

After several decades in the Midwest, Davis was restless. Starting in 1871, he, his American wife, and ten of their eleven children set off west in a covered wagon. By 1875, as they ambled through the Northwest, his wife finally announced that she had had enough and would go no further. They stopped in a pretty grove of trees with a stream flowing through, and founded the town of Cottonwood Springs. On this fortuitous site about halfway between Walla Walla and Spokane, the Davises bought 1,600 acres for $2.60 an acre, built a ten-room house, and then built a general store that doubled as a roadhouse with guest rooms and a recreation hall. The town was later renamed **Cashup** in honor of Davis's nickname: as one of the few people in the area to have real money, he made all the deals he could by offering "cash up front" or simply "cashup." In turn, he required cash payment whenever possible for the goods in his general store.

At the top of the nearby 3,610-foot butte, then called Pyramid Peak, Davis spent about $10,000 to build a road and a magnificent hotel with a wraparound balcony, and decorated it with locally grown wheat and furniture imported from England and the East Coast. The hotel burned down in 1911, after having stood idle since Davis's death in 1896. Eventually the peak was renamed Steptoe Butte, and then a geologist made an interesting discovery: The butte is actually the tip of a granite mountain more than 600 million years old, part of the Selkirk Range. The butte protrudes above the lava flows that cover the rest of the range, a mere 15 million years old. The word *steptoe* entered the language of geology, referring to the protrusion of an older formation above newer materials.

From Oakesdale the road follows the line of least resistance to the pleasant town of Tekoa, virtually on the Idaho state line. The road continues on north to Fairfield, and when you arrive here you are effectively out of the Palouse country and into the Spokane region. The difference is rainfall and topography. Here rainfall amounts are higher than in the Palouse country, and this leads to slightly different farming methods more rainfall means more weeds and at the same time greater crop yield. Lawn grass seed is a popular crop here. You'll also note that the timber is much thicker and more prevalent than in the Palouse.

The route ends when you reach I-90 in Opportunity.

Reardan to Sprague and the Floods

Estimated length: 85 miles
Estimated time: 3 hours

Getting there: From Reardan on US 2, go south on W231 to Sprague. Continue across I-90 on WA 23 to Colfax.

Highlights: You'll be in the heart of the Channeled Scablands, which occasioned a major geological debate in the early twentieth century. You'll see nice small towns with cafes rather than restaurants, and inexpensive, basic motels instead of inns, B&Bs, or hotels.

Time after time you'll hear people say they drove across eastern Washington and "didn't see a thing except more of nothing." This comment is particularly common among people who live in western Washington and think the only things worth seeing are trees, mountains, and saltwater. Poor souls.

True, much of eastern Washington is flat, and in the summer the scenery is bent and distorted out of shape by heat waves radiating upward from the fields and the pavement. But there is as much to see here as in western Washington if you know what to look for.

This trip over a little-used road is a good example. If July and August aren't your favorite travel months in the near desert of the wheat country,

This view of Edwall, taken late in an autumn afternoon, shows the peacefulness of the wheat country.

make this trip in the spring, while the wheat is still green and growing, or in the late fall, after the crop is harvested and the wheat for next year is just coming out of the ground like rows of tender grass.

If you're driving south from Reardan on WA 231, you will go across the same kind of landscape you have already been on, mainly rolling hills covered with wheat. You'll go through the picturesque town of Edwall, then climb up a series of low hills with Edwall nestled among the hills when you look back to the north.

A short distance further, you'll hit the western edge of the **Channeled Scabland,** which distinguishes Sprague from the rest of the wheat country. From here on east several miles, the landscape is a miniature canyon country, more barren and basalt-walled landscape than you've seen elsewhere in the area. An academic battle was fought for several decades over the Channeled Scabland, which deserves at least a brief discussion because it so completely changed contemporary geological thinking.

It is much easier to understand the Channeled Scabland when you fly over it in a small plane. This geological oddity is a series of dry channels that run generally south-southwest out of the Spokane area and fan out toward the Columbia River. For decades geologists simply assumed the channels were caused over a period of centuries by normal erosion from flowing water.

This was the accepted explanation until J. Harlen Bretz became interested in the area. He was a University of Chicago geology professor by way of Seattle. Long before Bretz became a professor, he was a high school biology teacher in Seattle with a deep interest in geology. Gradually geology took over his life until he finally gave up, got a Ph.D. from the University of Chicago in 1913, returned home and taught at the University of Washington, and eventually returned to teach at the University of Chicago for the rest of his career.

But his heart remained in Washington, specifically in the barren coulees and shiprocks of eastern Washington. The shape of the landscape nagged at him because he did not believe it was shaped by normal erosion. Then the first piece of the puzzle revealed itself.

"I saw a section of a topographic map and from that I got the idea," he said in a telephone interview in 1971, when he was 89 years old. He soon formulated the theory that the Channeled Scabland was not created by glacial activity and normal water erosion. Instead, he believed it was created by one or more catastrophic floods that originated from a vast lake dammed by earth and ice in the valley where Missoula, Montana, stands.

Bretz found more and more evidence to support his theory. He found lap marks high on the cliffs around Missoula, for example, and erratics—boulders carried far from their place of origin—high on the mountainsides along the Columbia River Gorge. Bretz believed the floods had occurred as the Ice Age waned, when melting snow and ice moved over the top of an earth-and-ice dam that might have been as high as 2,000 feet. When the dam broke, it released a 3,000-square-mile lake that contained half the volume of Lake Michigan, which is 500 cubic miles of water. The lake Bretz envisioned headed due west from Missoula across the Idaho Panhandle and down the Spokane Valley, where the natural contour of the land turned it south and west.

He believed that the Palouse River originally flowed down Washtucna Coulee where the towns of Washtucna and Kahlotus are now, and emptied into the Snake River about 70 miles further downstream from its present confluence at Lyons Ferry. Bretz believed that the first floods pounded in the Pasco basin and formed what he called Lake Lewis, filled the Yakima, Walla Walla, and Snake River valleys, and finally spilled over and bore into the Columbia River at Wallowa Gap. He believed the floods came through the gap up to 800 feet deep and at 1.66 cubic miles of water an hour for two or three weeks, or 190 times the greatest Columbia River flood on record.

The floods scoured the sides of the Columbia Gorge up to 1,000 feet high, and carried boulders from mountainsides or up valleys. When the flood hit the Willamette River, the wall of water headed upriver as far as Eugene and formed a temporary lake that covered up to 3,000 square miles. Bretz, most certainly a brave man, further annoyed his peers by saying these floods could have come through anywhere from six to 40 times.

This went completely against geologic thought at the time. Most geologic theory evolved in the 19th century, and was based in part on religion, which held strictly to the seven-day version of Creation given in the Bible. But slowly, at glacial speed, the theory of catastrophic events rather than gradual erosion came into acceptance. Then Bretz appeared in print saying the theory of catastrophe was valid in this case. When Ivy League scholars heard Bretz's theory, one snob called the University of Chicago "that Western trade school." They picked on the wrong man. Bretz was tenacious and he enjoyed a good academic brawl. So for several summers he worked in eastern Washington, gathering more ammunition for the battle. One by one he gained converts to his cause, especially from those who actually toured the area with him and came to imagine the roar of the floods.

It took 42 years for Bretz to be vindicated. It happened in 1965, when the International Geophysical Year was held in Denver. Bretz couldn't attend because of health problems, but he was well represented by a band of disciples who were determined that their point of view at least be seriously considered by an on-site examination. They arranged a trip across the West by chartered bus through the Rockies and into Montana, then down the course of the floods. At Missoula a Bretz believer began lecturing on what they were seeing from the bus windows and at specific stops for hikes. This continued all along the flood route. Finally, when the group stopped at a site near Kahlotus all the pieces of Bretz's theory fell into place: dry cataracts, the rerouting of the Palouse River, the stream beds that haven't seen running water in centuries, the ripple marks on canyon and coulee walls.

On that day most of his most outspoken opponents began backpedaling and some apologized to Bretz in print. And it was on that day that the group sent Bretz a long telegram of congratulations. At the end of the wire were the magic words: "We are all catastrophists!" Bretz was awarded the Penrose Medal, the Geological Society of America's highest award, in 1979, at the age of 96. Upon this occasion he told his son, "All my enemies are dead, so I have no one to gloat over." The J. Harlen Bretz Award is given annually to the most outstanding senior in the geology department at Albion College.

While driving across the Channeled Scabland you will occasionally see a ship-shaped hill rising over the scabland, always with the sharp end pointed northeast. This end will be sheer, while the other end of the rock will be rounded, and with dirt piled up against it. This was part of Bretz's proof that the floods washed away everything on one end and left soil on the southwest end. In addition, the southwest wind that blows almost every day of the year and brings in soil, called loess, has been steadily piling up on the southwest, blunted end.

If you drive beyond Sprague toward the Palouse Country, almost immediately you will almost immediately leave behind the Channeled Scabland and enter the Palouse. The change is dramatic. Instead of an occasional small patch of wheat among and between the rocks, you will suddenly be in the midst of vast fields of wheat. The houses, outbuildings and cars in the driveway will change from modest to expensive, and you will begin meeting very large and broad tractors on the backroads.

Eating and sleeping choices are slim to none on this route.

Towboats pushing barges along are a common sight on the Snake and Columbia Rivers.

CHAPTER

8

Down in the Snake River Canyon

Estimated length: 60 miles
Estimated time: 2 hours

Getting there: Take WA 193 west from Clarkston along the north side of the Snake River to WA 194, which curves back to Almota to make the steep descent back to the Snake River.

Highlights: You'll see the spectacular scenery of the Snake River Canyon, now reflected in the slack water behind dams, and the towboats and barges that run on the Snake to Clarkston-Lewiston.

I happened on this trip in the best of all possible ways: I saw the road marked on a map and took my chances because I had seen several sections of the Snake River in Washington, but hadn't been able to follow it any distance. This country-roads roulette procedure doesn't always work so well. I've found myself dead-ended in barnyards and on roads much too rough for a sedan. But this one was just fine.

All of the Snake River you'll see on this trip is slack water due to the series of dams that have turned the swift and treacherous river into calm water. It doesn't take a soaring imagination to get an idea of what the river was like before the dams. After reading accounts of travel on the Snake in those early days, it seems miraculous that anyone survived a trip on it.

The descent to the Snake River canyon is steep, no matter which route you choose.

The first accounts were those of Lewis and Clark, and the members of their party who kept their own journals. The group of 28 had almost frozen and starved to death while crossing the Bitterroot Mountains from the Missouri River headwaters into the Columbia River system (via the Clearwater River). When they finally arrived on the lower Clearwater, which empties into the Snake at Lewiston, the local Nez Perce gave them food, mostly dried salmon, which made some of the men extremely ill. Lewis and Clark urged the men on so they could get to the Pacific Ocean before the worst of winter arrived. Men who were very ill with abdominal cramps and the attendant inconveniences worked with the healthy to build canoes.

When the explorers launched their armada of unstable canoes, some of the men were too ill to do anything other than lie in the bottoms of the canoes, some of which swamped in the Snake. Nobody drowned, although some came close. Neither Lewis nor Clark was impressed with the scenery they were going through: It just meant a lot of work and discomfort to them.

DEATH OF A NEZ PERCE

The mouth of the Palouse River, where it empties into the Snake River, has apparently been occupied as long as any site in North America; it was here that the 8,000-year-old Mares Man was found, at that time the oldest human remains found in America.

The first white men to see the area were the Lewis and Clark Expedition, and they named the river in honor of George Drouillard, whose name they spelled Drewyer, when they passed it on October 13, 1805. They also found a large fishing village not far down the Snake, and out in a nearby meadow were several holes the Indians had dug for fish storage.

Eight years later a group of John Jacob Astor's fur trappers and traders were in the area and one of them committed an act against the friendly Nez Perce that would have consequences for years to come.

The man was John Clarke, who was given to pomposity and who carried with him a few pieces of nice clothing and, his most prized possession, a silver goblet. One of his greatest pleasures was drinking out of the goblet and letting his audience be impressed with the sight.

While he and his group were meeting with a Nez Perce band, Clarke produced his goblet, which he kept locked in a small case. The Indians were duly impressed, and Clarke poured a little wine in it and offered it to the chief, telling him that drinking wine from it would make him a better man. The chief was delighted, and it was passed from hand to hand around the campfire.

None of the Indians had seen such a sight before, and that night, for some reason, Clarke put it away in the case, but he forgot to lock it. The next morning it was gone. The case was open, and empty.

Clarke was enraged, and he called a meeting of the whole camp. He promised death to the man who stole it, and pleaded and cajoled as well. The Indians called a council and after discussing the matter, they called to Clarke. When he walked over to them, a chief produced the goblet from beneath his robe.

Clarke was obviously relieved, but still angry. He demanded to know who had stolen it, and when the Indians innocently produced him, Clarke proceeded to keep his word and strung up a rope to hang him.

The Indians naturally disagreed. They believed that when a man produces something he has stolen, forgiveness is in order and he is exonerated of the sin. But Clarke insisted on keeping his word, in spite of the pleadings.

He built a gallows of poles from the Indian's own lodge, and hung him. Up until the moment they found that the man was really dead the Indians believed he would be cut down with the close call a moral lesson. But when they cut him down and found that he was dead, the Indians mounted their horses and rode off in all directions to tell everyone of the deed.

It took almost a year, but in April of 1814 a party of trappers found the Indian widow and children of another trapper, Pierre Dorion, down near the mouth of the Snake. The previous January the Nez Perce had massacred her husband and several other trappers, told her it was in retaliation for Clarke's hanging the previous June. She and her two sons had managed to survive the winter in the Blue Mountains.

That was the assessment of many early settlers, and when the steamboats began working the Snake, the toll in human lives, boats, barges, and freight was enormous. The major cargo was grain from the rich fields of the Palouse country. Even with the problems, shipping by boat and barge was much cheaper than by rail. It still is, which is why you'll see so many barges along the river.

Like Lewis and Clark, the pioneer shippers and growers weren't thrilled by the river scenery. The more beautiful it was, the more it seemed to cost them, as it was just plain difficult to get the grain aboard the barges. Only a few places were flat enough to permit the horse-drawn wagons of grain to come right to the river's edge. With most of the river's course through the best wheat-growing area running down in deep, steep canyons, the growers and shippers tried transporting the grain from the roads above to the river below by means of chutes. This didn't work well because the friction ground the grain into flour or meal. Much of what arrived at the bottom was wheat dust. Newer chutes were built that controlled the speed of the grain, but nothing worked as well as it should have. Finally trucks came onto the scene, which made it more practical to haul the grain longer distances to a decent landing.

Today only an occasional board or groove in the canyon walls reminds us of the chutes. Enormous storage tanks and elevators store the grain until it can be transported downriver. When the settlers began filling the higher ground, others were forced to try the river bottom. They found small protected areas that we now call microclimates in the canyons. Some of these were perfect for growing fruit. So many orchards grew in the area that it became a tradition for people from all over the area to go down to the orchards to pick their own fruit. Unfortunately, many of the original orchards were victims of the flooding behind the dams.

During all of those pioneer years steamboats were the only form of transportation in the Snake canyon, but in 1908 a railroad was opened between Riparia and Lewiston. Before long a rough road was built along the tracks for horse-drawn vehicles, then automobiles.

The canyon is really tame now—you'll find no white water and its roads are even better than before. When the Lower Granite Dam's floodgates closed in 1974, it flooded the canyon there to a depth of 80 feet. The Army Corps of Engineers had to build new roadbeds for both the highway and the railroad. Unfortunately, on the first part of this trip the railroad is between the highway and the river, but later on the paved highway and railroad switch sides and several turnouts were built so you can stop and watch the towboats bringing the barges around the innumerable twists and turns of the canyon.

Grain elevators are as common in Eastern Washington as mushrooms are in Western Washington.

The road suddenly takes a sharp right turn and heads north through a V-shaped canyon and soon emerges on the wheat plateau. If you stay on the same road, it will take you into Pullman.

Sunburned hills and dark scrub brush, mixed with an occasional grove of trees, are common in the Klickitat Valley just off the gorge.

CHAPTER

9

Exploring the Columbia River Gorge

Estimated length: 200 miles
Estimated time: 1–2 days

Getting there: If you're going through Vancouver, go south on I-5 and take Exit 1 to WA 14 east. If you skip downtown Vancouver and the parks, take Exit 7 from the I-205 bypass route that goes east of Vancouver and connect with WA 14 about six miles upriver from I-5, well beyond the heavy urban traffic. The entire route discussed here is on WA 14, which ends 200 miles away when it connects with I-82 and US 395.

Highlights: You'll see Fort Vancouver National Historical Site, Old Apple Tree Park, small and sometimes quirky towns, towboats and barges on the Columbia River, sailboarders on the river, waterfalls and mountain scenery, excellent resorts, and one of the most unusual museums in the Northwest.

Begin this trip at Fort Vancouver, where the Hudson's Bay Company had its outpost through the middle of the nineteenth century. The **Fort Vancouver National Historic Site** is off I-5 just before you reach the Columbia River. The fort is almost an exact replica of the original that shows how the trappers and Hudson's Bay factors lived when the British and Americans were jockeying for power and territory. This was one of the most important sites in the history of the Pacific Northwest because it was the unofficial goal of many Americans migrating across the plains and mountains to the Oregon Country. Many of them arrived at the post without much more than they were wearing because their route down the Columbia River was one of the worst parts of the trip across the plains to the ocean: In those days the Columbia was an incredibly wild and dangerous river as it went through the gorge. There were rapids, hundreds of rocks to dodge, waterfalls and eddies. Rafts upset, people and horses drowned, and goods disappeared beneath the deep water. It was rare for a party to go through the gorge without losing something or someone. When they at last arrived at civilization, as represented by Fort Vancouver, they were always in need of something, especially food and seeds or seedlings to begin their new lives.

Although he was under orders to strongly discourage Americans from settling in the region, Dr. John McLoughlin, the gruff and scowling chief factor of Fort Vancouver, was much too kind and generous for the good of Hudson's Bay Company, and he helped the newcomers as much as he could. All the while the Hudson's Bay Company was doing what it could to discourage the Americans. One of their most dramatic efforts was taking a scorched-earth policy toward trapping. The company tried to "trap out" the beaver population in Washington and Oregon, hoping it would discourage settlers. But most settlers were not trappers, so the policy affected very few of the newcomers.

Eventually McLoughlin was fired for his humanitarian efforts. He lived out the remainder of his life quietly in Oregon City with his Native American wife amid Americans. Finally the Americans won the boundary dispute and the English had to withdraw to what is now Canada. Some locals think the Canadians got their revenge by naming their city Vancouver, which grew much larger than the American Vancouver.

Fort Vancouver is almost surrounded by remnants of the **Vancouver Barracks,** an army post built later by Americans. The post would hardly be known to anyone today were it not for the service of a lowly, lonely lieutenant named Ulysses S. Grant, who served there a few years before the Civil War broke out. Vancouver has an elegance about it, thanks to the row of Vancouver Barracks officers' residences and other Victorian-era buildings, that hasn't been diminished by the heavy commuter traffic between it and Portland.

Almost directly beneath the Interstate bridge on Columbia Way is one of the state's most interesting trees. Planted in 1826, this pampered specimen of an **English greening apple** is believed to be the first apple tree brought to the Pacific Northwest. In its heyday (if it even had one) it was used as a baking apple, and also for horse feed. Yet it has been elevated to icon status and is generally considered the matriarch of Washington's apple industry,

The annual Old Apple Tree Festival is typically held on the first Saturday in October from 10 to 2. The festival focuses on environmental education and historic preservation with Heritage Tree walks, Historic Clark County tours, a birds of prey show, scavenger hunts along the waterfront trail, and other kids' activities. All activities are free, and as a bonus, the Urban Forestry Commission gives each visitor free state-grown apples and tree cuttings from the Old Apple Tree. From Vancouver, take WA 14 east through Camas and Washougal. Compared with the fast, level I-84 that runs along the river on the Oregon side, State 14 is a country road. It is two-lane and very crooked as it follows the contours of the land rather than slicing through. The Columbia River is within sight for most of this journey. The highway is for drivers who have some extra time to spend on the road; those in a hurry will cross into Oregon and zoom along I-84.

Although neither Camas nor Washougal is yet a destination town, you might want to stop in Washougal for a self-guided tour of the **Pendleton Woolen Mills** factory, or visit the Pendleton factory shop at 2 17th Street, a combination retail store and outlet where you can buy clothing and bedding at reduced rates.

Just east of Washougal you will enter the 292,000-acre **Columbia River Gorge National Scenic Area,** created in 1986 to protect the scenic, cultural, recreational, and natural resources of the gorge while encouraging growth only in urban areas. The scenic area created a partnership between the forest service, a commission made up on local citizens to oversee the gorge, the Indian tribes, and six local counties. For some 70 miles the scenic area takes in both sides of the river, ending on the Washington side at the Mayhill Museum near US 97. As with all government programs that limit the uses of private land, the designated scenic area remains controversial among some locals, but its popularity continues to grow with visitors.

The first of many places to stop to enjoy the scenery is Cape Horn, with a view many miles upriver that will give you an idea of what you will see along the way. **Beacon Rock State** Park is next and it stands more than 800 feet tall, the largest monolith of its kind in America. This former volcano plug became a state park after it was almost destroyed when the man who owned it wanted to turn it into a vertical rock quarry. You can climb to its summit on steps with handrails, but be warned that it is a long and steep climb.

From the rock you can see Bonneville Dam, the first of the series of dams that changed the Columbia forever. All of the river's immense falls, a series of cascades, deadly rapids, and whirlpools were covered by the chain of hydroelectric dams that stretch from Bonneville upstream into Canada. Only one stretch of the Columbia still flows freely in Washington, a 60-mile section called Hanford Reach that was protected only because it now falls within the Hanford Nuclear Reservation.

It may seem strange, but the river is so wide and deep that the effect of tides on the ocean could be felt up to Cello Falls, near where the Bonneville Dam was built. Today the dam is where the effect of the ocean tides stops, roughly 130 miles upriver from Astoria. This is also where boats, towboats, and barges start going through a series of locks to make their way upriver. You will see many towboats pushing a group of barges up and down the river, hauling grain to Portland or beyond, taking fuel upriver, and carrying many other kinds of cargo. The towboats and barges have been built especially for the locks and fit them exactly. A load, called a "lockage," on the Columbia is much smaller than those on the Mississippi, where a lockage may be a quarter of a mile long. In contrast, the Columbia River locks limit the lockage's to 630 feet long and 84 feet wide.

Barges are the most economical means of moving freight. As an example, to move 3,500 tons of grain downriver, it would take 116 semi trailers or 35 railcars. However, only one towboat and one barge can do the job for about half the price truckers must charge.

Much of the colorfulness of river travel disappeared when the dams were built. Excitement and danger still exist for boatmen, and the wind, snow, and rain are as uncomfortable as they always were. But before the dams, boatmen had special skills that enabled them to navigate a line of barges on the swift current and among the rocks that, with one bit of poor judgment, could cause the barges to stack up on rocks or sink. Many of the rocks in the river were named for tug skippers who missed a crucial turn in a spectacular fashion. One story that persists is about a skipper who, in the vernacular of the profession, stacked up his barges on the bank of the Snake River. When he was asked what happened, he said that he had always used the two doors of a barn as a beacon: when he could see all the way through the barn by both doors of, he knew it was time to begin his turn.

"Somebody closed the barn doors," he lamented.

One of the smallest towns in Washington is Skamania, which is mostly a single building that houses the post office, grocery, and general store. It is a good place to stock up on snacks and souvenirs.

Stevenson is the next town, small and unpretentious, with a good county museum. It is the county seat of Skamania County and earned a degree of fame for being the first government to pass a law making it a crime to kill a Sasquatch, or Bigfoot. Although few members of the county council really believed the creature existed, they wanted to take no chances if one should be found. The initial law was passed in 1969 and later amended but the protection remains.

Stevenson is the first of a cluster of towns, some no more than a building or two, built in the heart of the Cascade Range. Others are Home Valley, Cook, Underwood, White Salmon, and Bingen. Lodging is often difficult to find along here because the few places to stay are so popular, such as Carson Hot Springs, where guests come year after year for the mineral baths and solitude. The Skamania Lodge is a major destination resort. Both are discussed at the end of the chapter.

From White Salmon eastward the scenery changes rapidly from the damp, evergreen forests of western Washington to the dry, open country of eastern Washington. The geology becomes more stark and dramatic as old lava flows appear in the form of basaltic cliffs and outcroppings. From here eastward basalt in all its shapes, sizes, and colors dominates the landscape.

Two north-south highways join State 14 along here: Forest Service Road 30 comes down the Wind River from the Gifford Pinchot National Forest near Mount St. Helens, and State 141 comes down from Trout Lake and Mount Adams. An interesting alternate trip is to take State 141 north to Trout Lake, then follow the paved county road east to the cowboy town of Glenwood and back down to the Columbia River on State 142, a route described in the Forest Service Road 23 trip (chapter 11).

Soon after leaving the small town of Bingen you'll be in open country, extremely hot in the summer and extremely cold in the winter. You'll already have noted the strong wind that blows almost constantly through the gorge, sort of an enormous regional breathing as the air rushes back and forth through the Cascades, depending on the pressure systems on either side of the mountains. The gorge is one of the best places in the world for windsurfing, and world championship competitions are held

LEWIS AND CLARK

They were a sad sight when they came down the Clearwater River out of Idaho and into the Snake River. Almost everyone was ill. They had almost starved and froze to death coming over the Bitterroot Mountains in deep snow, and when they reached the lower Clearwater River, the friendly Nez Perce fed them dried fish, camas roots and hawthorne berries. The food almost killed the men, and some were too sick to walk for days to come.

It was September 1805, and Meriwether Lewis and William Clark knew they had to keep going in order to reach the Pacific Ocean before winter set in. They set about building their five canoes. A chief named Twisted Hair befriended the men and was of great help to them. He showed them how to burn out the ponderosa pine logs—Lewis and Clark preferred to chop them out, but most of the men lay in tents and makeshift shelters, curled in the fetal position with cramps and diarrhea. Clark thought perhaps the illness, from which he also suffered and described clearly in his journal, was due to a change in diet from red meat to fish and berries, rather than poisoning. So he sent their best hunter, George Drouillard, in search of red meat. He came back shortly with a deer. Some of the men felt better a few hours after they ate it and were able to go to work building their flotilla.

Chief Twisted Hair offered to take care of their 38 horses during their absence, and since the Nez Perce horses, the famous appaloosa, were so superior to the animals the explorers bought in the mountains, there was little fear of their being stolen. They marked the horses by braiding their manes in a particular way, and left. They launched the dugout canoes on October 7 into the rapid-filled Clearwater. Some of the men were still too weak to paddle and were little more than dead weight in the bottom of the crude craft. One canoe hit a boulder the second day and sank. The others careened crazily in the swift and cold water.

Where they once had traveled for days without seeing an Indian, from the confluence of the Clearwater into the Snake, all the way down the Columbia to the sea, they were never out of sight of Indians.

On the fifth day out they reached the worst rapids yet, a set that ran two miles and was called the Texas Rapids before being covered with backwaters from a dam. Some Indians led them through in a canoe with no casualties, and two days later they ran another set without mishap. Finally, on October 16, they entered the Columbia River. They celebrated their entry into the major river by stopping to converse with a gathering of about two hundred Indians. They also bought seven dogs for dinner. According to entries in their journals, the party bought at least 50 dogs for food on the expedition. The Indians didn't think much of their diet, and when they returned upriver the following spring, an Indian threw a puppy and an insult at Lewis, who came close to killing the man.

Although the Columbia was far larger than the other rivers they had navigated since leaving the Missouri, it was by far the most treacherous because its rapids were much more powerful with the weight of so much water on them, and the Columbia Gorge had everything from ripples to giant waterfalls. They portaged around the worst, such as Celilo Falls, and when they reached the falls at the mouth of the Deschutes River, they were attacked by so many fleas that the men had to strip down naked while making the portage so they could more easily brush the insects off.

The Indians along the lower portion of the gorge had been in contact with white men before, and had lost whatever awe and respect they may have had originally. They tried to steal anything they could put their hands on, and Clark had a pipe tomahawk stolen during a parlay with them. While he searched every man for it, someone stole a coat. They found the coat, but Clark was "much displeased with those fellows, which they discovered and moved off on their return home to their village." The explorers loaded into the canoe again and continued drifting toward the ocean.

"We are all wet cold and disagreeable, rain continues & increases." This sentence could have been used to describe every day of their voyage from late October until the following spring when they returned upriver and at last entered the desertland of the middle Columbia.

On November 7, Clark wrote "Great joy in camp we are in view of the ocean." But they weren't quite there yet. A wind had picked up during the night and created waves that came crashing onto the shoreline where they camped. Actually, they still had about 20 miles to go. They looked for a suitable campsite on the north side of the river mouth, but the land was too open and they found no game for food. So they looked across the river. Finally, on December 8 they settled on a place to build what would become Fort Clatsop near Astoria, Oregon, on a river later named for Lewis and Clark. The fort wasn't completed until December 30, and the men spent Christmas wishing for a feast rather than enjoying one because the wildlife was hard to find in the thick coastal forest.

When they later reviewed entries in their meticulous diaries, they found that during five months they spent at Fort Clatsop, only 12 days were without rain. They slept under blankets infested with fleas, and their Christmas dinner "concisted of pore Elk, so much Spoiled that we eate it thro' mear necessity." They continued to eat elk for weeks, until they bought a basket of the oily smelt, a type of candlefish, from the Clatsops which Clark said, with great relief and gusto, were "superior to any fish I ever tasted."

They were the first white men on record to descend the Columbia River from the Snake confluence to the Pacific. But they weren't the first to visit the mouth of the river because they found a Clatsop woman with the name J. Bowman tattooed on her arm, and some suffered venereal diseases brought there by white men.

The Lewis and Clark Expedition of 1804–06 was the catalyst that stretched America's boundaries from sea to sea. Where other politicians had been content to take the fledging country a little farther west at a time, President Thomas Jefferson wanted the whole thing. The Louisiana Purchase gave the United States all of the Great Plains and most of the Rocky Mountains, but that left the West Coast in Spanish and English hands. The Lewis and Clark Expedition whetted Congress's appetite for more land, and as a result the Pacific Coast from Washington down to California was eventually added to the map of the United States.

---

along here each year. Since the water and air are so cold, nearly every windsurfer wears a wet or dry suit while they dart like water bugs among the towboat and other river traffic.

Keep an eye out for the **Maryhill Museum** just before the intersection with US 97, the major north-south highway that runs from Canada to California. This is one of the nation's most eccentric museums, and one of the best in the Northwest, in spite of its remote location. The museum began as a desert palace for a multimillionaire named Samuel Hill (Yes, the expression "What in Sam Hill!" came from him). He married Mary Hill, daughter of the railroad magnate James J. Hill, and she didn't have to go to the bother of learning a new surname. Sam Hill bought about 7,000 acres of land for his castle and tried to lure a group of Quakers to start a colony there. The Quakers didn't bite. Neither did his wife, Mary, in spite of his naming the place in her honor. Apparently she never even visited it. After living on Seattle's Queen Anne Hill a few years, she moved to Washington, D.C., and reveled in the social scene there. She apparently did not come back to the Northwest, and Hill seldom, if ever, visited her in Washington, D.C.

Hill made himself a moving target during his full life. He conceived of the Peace Arch at the U.S.-Canadian border at Blaine and got school

The Maryhill Museum is one of the most eccentric museums in the state, and well worth the long drive.   Maryhill Museum

children involved in the fundraising and construction. He was largely responsible for construction of the beautiful old Columbia Gorge Highway on the Oregon side, which is now being restored; he even underwrote it with his own money, first sending his engineer to Europe to study how roads were built through the Alps. After World War I, President Wilson appointed Hill to a commission to help rebuild Europe, and it was then that he met two women who became important in his life. The first was an American dancer named Loie Fuller, who introduced him around Paris, even to the sculptor Auguste Rodin. He also befriended Queen Marie of Romania while helping her with funds to rebuild her country.

After numerous mishaps and failed opportunities, Hill decided to turn his mostly completed sagebrush palace into a museum. Queen Marie had time on her hands, so she came to dedicate the building in 1926, trailed on her transcontinental rail journey by newsmen with lots of unanswered questions regarding her friendship with Hill. She also brought boxcar loads of furniture, thrones, clothing, jewelry, and religious objects from her vast horde. This trove was joined by a vast collection of Auguste Rodin sculpture and watercolors, and a rare collection of miniature French fashion mannequins. Hill died in 1931 before the museum could be completed, but another wealthy friend, Anna Speckles of the sugar dynasty, took over and completed the place. She donated many pieces from her extensive art collection to the cause and saw to it that the museum opened in 1940. It has been open ever since and is supported in part by leases on the estate surrounding it. In addition to the collections already described, the museum houses a major collection of regional Indian artifacts.

Three miles upriver from the museum is still another Hill gift. He had a **reconstruction of Stonehenge** built overlooking the Columbia. He dedicated it to the war dead from Klickitat County, and ordered that he be buried in a crypt just below the Stonehenge copy.

Just after State 14 crosses US 97, you will see a sign warning you that you won't find gasoline or food for 80 miles. This stretch is obviously very lonely, but it is a good highway and the scenery is open, with outcroppings of basalt lining the two-lane blacktop and the river below. The route is hilly in places, but the drive is fast because traffic is almost always light. At the end of the 80 miles, State 14 runs into I-82 at Plymouth. High on the windswept hill above the river and near the intersection is the Columbia Crest Winery, one of the largest, if not the largest, in eastern Washington. The winery has a visitors' area where you can watch part of the winemaking process, and a large gift shop where you can buy wine, picnic supplies and gifts.

From here you can take a sharp turn north on I-82 through the Horse Heaven Hills to the Tri-Cities, or turn south and cross the Columbia River into Oregon.

IN THE AREA

Accommodations

Bonneville Hot Springs Resort & Spa, 1252 E. Cascade Dr., North Bonneville. Call 866-459-1678 or 509-427-7767. This luxury hotel set back in the deep forest is operated like a European spa with luxurious rooms, an excellent restaurant, and hot mineral springs for soaking. Web site: www.bonnevilleresort.com.

Joslyn House B&B, 706 W. Steuben, Bingen. Call (509) 493-4888. Built in 1860, this landmark house is an easy walk from the only AMTRAK station in the Columbia Gorge. It has seven rooms, all with shared bath, plus an outdoor hot tub and a TV room. Web site: www.bingenhaus.com

Mt. Adams Lodge at the Flying L Ranch, 25 Flying L Lane, Glenwood. Call 509-364-3488. This resort is a short distance off the gorge, but so remote in some ways that it could be hundreds of miles from the busy river. It has no Internet access, nor does it have cell phone reception. But the owners quickly point out on their Web site that they do have "a Frisbee disc golf course, great mountain views, wildflowers, birds," and so forth. Web site: www.mt-adams.com

Skamania Lodge, P.O. Box 189, 1131 S.W. Skamania Lodge Way, Stevenson. Call 509-427-7700. Built in 1993 by an unusual public–private partnership of the Columbia River Gorge Commission, the USDA Forest Service, Skamania County, and Greco Resources, Inc., the Skamania Lodge was designed to resemble the lodges built in many national parks around the turn of the 20th century: high-pitched roofs, black wrought iron, and large timbers, some more than a century old, recycled from a Bumble Bee cannery in Astoria, Oregon. The lodge has 254 guest rooms, all with in-house movies, video games, and room service. Web site: www.skamania.com

Attractions and Recreation

Columbia Crest Winery, Hwy 221 (Columbia Crest Dr.), Paterson. Call 509-875-2061.

Columbia River Gorge National Scenic Area, 902 Wasco Ave., Hood River, OR. Call 503-386-2333.

Fort Vancouver National Historical Site, 612 E. Reserve St., Vancouver. Call 360-816-6230. The fort is open throughout the year except January 1, November 25, and December 24–25 and 31. The entrance fee is $3 per person or $5 per family.

Mayhill Museum, 35 Mayhill Dr., Goldendale. Call 509-773-3733. The museum is open seven days a week, including all holidays, from 9 to 5, March 15–November 15. General admission is $7, seniors $6, children (ages 6–16) $2.

Mont Elise Winery, 315 Steuben, Bingen. Call 509-493-3000.

Pendleton Woolen Mills Outlet, 2 17th St., Washougal. Call 360-835-1118.

The Bluebirds of Bickleton

Estimated length: 33 miles to Sunnyside from Bickleton: 69 miles to Sunnyside from Goldendale via Bickleton
Estimated time: 1–3 hours

Getting there: Take WA 241 south from Sunnyside to Mabton and Bickleton.

Highlights: You'll travel over the Horse Heaven Hills, which were officially named in 1881 by James Kinney, a Yakima pioneer, in 1857. (After seeing the knee-high grass of these hills for the first time, he exclaimed, "This is surely a horse heaven!") Hundreds of birdhouses in Bickleton show the town's great dedication has to preserving habitat for bluebirds.

If you like your spaces wide open and unpopulated, this long drive from Goldendale to the Yakima Valley will make your vacation. One thing to remember about driving in eastern Washington is that the landscape isn't as predictable as one might think, given that the climate is very dry east of the Cascade Mountains. While everything may look much alike, be prepared for endless and surprising subtleties. Here you'll find miles and miles of arid tan, but, suddenly, you look "over there" you see a small zone of wetness and greenery only a meteorologist can explain. This is what you can expect driving northeast out of Goldendale toward Bickleton, Cleveland,

This is the most popular and accurate image of Bickleton: bluebird houses everywhere and in a variety of shapes.

and the Yakima Valley. The landscape itself is beautiful and rolling, with several steep canyons to surprise you as you cruise along.

Before you go off on the cross-country trek, stop for a look around **Goldendale**. It is a pleasant farming community with enough elevation to have timber. It is close enough to the Columbia River and the Mount Adams backcountry to have lakes and streams nearby for fishing and boating. It has an excellent county museum and several Victorian-era homes and public buildings that are kept in good condition. A small observatory is on a hill outside of town and when an eclipse is scheduled for the Northwest, thousands of people flock to the hillsides and farms to camp overnight and watch the show.

The road to Bickleton begins climbing immediately after leaving Goldendale and levels off on top of a plateau. Oak trees grow in the canyons and in the gullies leading off the road. Instead of only wheat and hay, you will usually find at least one sunflower farm along the route. For the most part, the road travels through unpopulated country. It is paved until it reaches a stretch of broken landscape. Here the road drops down into Badger Gulch where a series of creeks, dry most of the year, merge to become Rock Creek. After the road winds back up on top again, the pavement returns.

The first community of any size is Cleveland, which was settled in 1879 by a man from that Ohio city. It has a rather grand cemetery near the road and a cluster of houses, but no businesses. Just a short distance along the road is the only real town in the area, Bickleton. Here you will find small, one-story buildings in the Western style, a grocery store, a tavern, a few other businesses typical of small farm and ranch towns, and some well-maintained churches. Bickleton was settled the same year as Cleveland and named for its founder, Charles N. Bickle, who delivered mail for several years between his home and Goldendale, a two-day horseback trip each way.

Today Bickleton is best known as the bluebird capital of the Northwest, or even the world. This is because several hundred birdhouses are scattered throughout the town and surrounding countryside to serve as homes for the large number of bluebirds that come there year after year, and have been coming since long before the area was settled by white men. Why this species selected that region for their summer home remains a mystery. Once settlers arrived and began clearing timber for buildings and to make way for crops, the bluebird population naturally dwindled. Nobody thought much about it until, sometime in the 1960s, a couple from Richland, Washington, Jess and Elva Brinkerhoff, came up to Bickleton to see the wildflowers that bloomed profusely each spring. The family became aware of the dwindling bluebird population and knew that this species builds nests only in existing cavities. On that day Jess Brinkerhoff built a birdhouse, using a gallon can he found in a nearby dump. Bluebirds moved in almost moments after he mounted the can on a tree.

That was the beginning of a lifelong occupation for the family. The next year the Brinkerhoffs appeared in Bickleton with nine birdhouses they had built, and asked permission from farmers and homeowners to place the birdhouses on fenceposts and trees. Permission was always granted, and for the next 30 years the Brinkerhoffs brought more birdhouses to the area. The only real birdhouse census taken was several years ago, when more than 2,500 were counted. The tradition continues and is a normal part of daily life in Bickleton.

Bickleton has another unusual tradition, this one involving a carousel. The 1905 Herschell-Spillman carousel, purchased in 1929 in Portland, is believed to be only one of three still in operation. It is brought out of storage once a year and assembled for the Alder Creek Pioneer Picnic held each June.

The road continues through ranches and occasional farms beyond Bickleton. Then, dramatically, it drops over the crest of a steep hill, and there, laid out before you, is the Yakima Valley, green and inviting after the dry scenery of the drive. The road curves and switchbacks its way to the valley floor, then makes a straight run toward the small town of Mabton—and onward to Sunnyside.

The Forest Service maintains this beautiful road that runs north-south between Mt. St. Helens and Mt. Adams.

CHAPTER

11

Between the Volcanoes on Road 23

Estimated lengths: 56 miles from Randle to Trout Lake; 72 miles from Randle to Glenwood; 107 miles from Randle to Goldendale
Estimated time: 3 hours

Getting there: Take Forest Service Road 23 from Randle on WA 12 south to Trout Lake, then go east on the Trout Lake–Glenwood Road to Glenwood. Continue from Glenwood down to the Klickitat River canyon and WA 142, which will take you to Goldendale.

Highlights: This trip offers some of the very best views of Mount St. Helens, Mount Rainier, and Mount Adams, secluded lakes, dense forests, remote small towns, quiet inns, horseback riding, and hiking.

When Mount St. Helens blew its top on May 18, 1980, killed 59 people, and created a wasteland of fallen trees covered with ash, the first version of this book was sitting on the printing press waiting for the printers to come back to work on Monday. When I heard that the mountain had blown laterally rather than vertically and had leveled thousands of square acres of Gifford Pinchot National Forest, my first thought was not the fate of the book but of the road—Forest Service Road 23—that runs from WA 12 at Randle south to Trout Lake near the Columbia Gorge.

This is one of the most beautiful drives through any national forest in

Washington. The road is paved all the way through the forest, and it goes so close to Mount Adams that you are likely to think you can hit it with a rock. But the map doesn't lie; it is still 20 miles away. One of the many bonuses of the route is the short side trip to the top of Burley Mountain, which has a panoramic view of all four volcanoes—Mount Rainier, Mount Adams, Mount Hood in Oregon and, of course, Mount St. Helens, which is the closest. Unlike some government roads in remote places, Road 23 is well marked at each intersection. Sometimes it degenerates to a single lane with frequent widened spots so cars and trucks can peacefully coexist, but most of it is two-lane blacktop.

To see the view from atop Burley Mountain, turn left off Road 23 on the road to Tower Rock Campground and continue to the BURLEY MOUNTAIN sign. The dirt road is seven miles of switchbacks through the thick timber before emerging on top and straightening out a bit. The 5,300-foot summit of Burley Mountain has the remains of an old lookout tower. The road continues southward and drops back down into the forest and eventually merges with a main route through the forest. The summit is a wonderful place to have a good, long look around at the summit to admire the four volcanoes and to be glad you weren't standing there on Sunday, May 18, 1980, when **Mount St. Helens** exploded, creating 300-mile-an-hour winds that carried temperatures of more than 300 degrees Fahrenheit.

Until this happened, St. Helens was almost a perfect cone and was sometimes called America's Mount Fuji. Spirit Lake at its northeast base, was a popular camping area and millions of photographs had been taken of the mountain reflected in the lake. However, in March 1980, the mountain began a series of small eruptions, steam and ash puffs that rose several thousand feet in the air. More ominously, the eastern side of the mountain began bulging and scientists on the site knew it was only a matter of time before the mountain would literally blow its top. It did so at 8:32 a.m. on Sunday, May 18. The blast took off 1,400 feet of the mountain and the ash cloud climbed 16 miles into the sky and drifted east, bringing darkness at noon to many eastern Washington towns, including Yakima, Moses Lake, Ritzville, Spokane, and parts of Idaho and Montana. Ashes covered everything and the hardest-hit town was Ritzville where you can still faintly see traces of the ash along roadsides and ditches. The ashes had a high obsidian (glass) content and the glass was very hard on machinery. But the benefits were that the ash enriched the soil and crops since have benefited from this unexpected and unwelcome natural fertilizer.

The benign and rounded summit of Mt. Adams is very often in sight as you drive along Forest Service Road 23.

The eruption created enormous flash floods of melted snow and ice that swept down the mountainside into small rivers, which became big rivers and eventually emptied into the Columbia. Ship traffic was halted on the Columbia until dredges could open the channels again. Major tributaries, such as the Cowlitz River, were clogged and all along the Cowlitz River today are mounds of debris dredged from the river in 1980.

Back to Burley Mountain, one of the nicest views from the summit is of the series of mountains that are different shades of blue depending on their distance from you. They undulate off into the distance, becoming fainter and fainter with each ridge. After enjoying this view, it will be time to backtrack down the mountain to Road 23 and continue the southward journey so you can arrive in Trout Lake or the Columbia Gorge before dark.

Most of the drive through the Cascade forest is usually uneventful because the road is so well maintained. An occasional Forest Service campground has been built along the way, and there is a cluster of them just

Road 23 is very picturesque.

north of the border of the **Mount Adams Wilderness Area.** These lakes and campgrounds—Olallie Lake, Chain of Lakes, and Takhlakh—have excellent views of Mount Adams and are among the most popular car campgrounds in the national forest. You can try for a campsite but don't be surprised if they're all taken, especially in midsummer.

As an aside, on my first trip down Road 23 I stopped at Lake Takhlakh to take a photo of Mount Adams looming over it, and noticed a lot of activity on the edge of the lake. I walked down and found that my visit had coincided with the moment tadpoles become frogs. Dozens of the tadpoles-with-legs were emerging from the water onto dry land, apparently for the first time. It was a strange feeling to watch all those little critters coming out of the water, apparently oblivious to the large mammal watching them.

Occasionally you will see the 12,276-foot Mount Adams through the timber, but you haven't seen a snow-capped volcano until you've rounded the curve near Council Lake. There you will see Adams looming up above you, looking as benign as a big ice cream cone. As Northwest volcanoes go, "benign" is a good description of Mount Adams. It hasn't erupted in recorded history, although it is still active. It is also easy to climb, as 12,000-foot peaks go. Climbing it requires very little in the way of technical skills, and in good weather the climb isn't much more than a long uphill hike.

An unusual aspect of this part of the Cascade Mountains is the abundance of wild huckleberries that grow in this particular forest. During August and into September, berry pickers by the hundred can be seen in the woods along these roads, picking the succulent berries. They are of special significance to the Yakima Indians, whose reservation shares this part of the Cascade Range forest. The Yakima tribe has exclusive rights to huckleberries in many parts of the forest and when pickers obtain the required permits at Forest Service offices, they are given maps that clearly show where they can and cannot pick.

The road meanders through the forest, and, at one point, skirts around the edge of a mountainside with steep drop-offs to give the faint of heart mild acrophobia. Eventually it eases down to level land, and suddenly you are in the small town of Trout Lake, where you can get gas for your car and food for yourself in a cafe at the main intersection. Gifford Pinchot National Forest has a ranger station on the western edge of town.

The main route continues south to the Columbia River, but for a continuation of scenic beauty, take the road that leads due east from Trout Lake to Glenwood on an unmarked county road. The road takes off east from WA 23 just north of Trout Lake, and passes several well-tended ranches and hay farms before beginning a slight climb above the valley to cross a low divide. The drive to Glenwood is uneventful as it crosses mainly flat land with a few trees. You'll occasionally see Mount Adams off to the northwest, and Mount Hood across the Columbia River to the south.

Glenwood is very small and has a cowboy flavor to it, because the dense timber of Gifford Pinchot National Forest has been left behind and the landscape is more John Ford Western than Paul Bunyan lumberjack. The Cascade Range has been left behind and the rainfall has dropped dramatically.

Just east of Glenwood, the road reaches the **Klickitat River** canyon and pine forests that feel more spacious than the claustrophobic Cascade forests. The road skirts the edge of the sheer basaltic cliffs, and the highway department has built only an occasional turnout so we can enjoy the view of the deep canyon. Eventually the road crosses the Klickitat and climbs slowly up the northern side of the canyon. This road gives you great views of the surrounding countryside, and an occasional thrill when a logging truck comes barreling down the highway flinging chunks of bark, gravel, and dust. When the road emerges from the rough hills along the Klickitat, it joins WA 142 a short distance from Goldendale.

IN THE AREA

Attractions and Recreation

Gifford Pinchot National Forest, Randle District. Call 360-497-1100.

Mount St. Helens National Volcanic Monument Headquarters, 42218 N.E. Yale Bridge Rd., Amboy. Call 360-449-7800.

CHAPTER

12

Ambling through the Wine Country

Estimated length: 70 to 150 miles

Estimated time: 1 day to 1 week, depending on how many wineries and towns you want to visit.

Getting there: Take I-10 to Ellensburg, then I-82 south to Selah. From Selah down through the valley you'll zigzag back and forth along the Yakima River on Highways 97, 22, and 12 and assorted country roads, some paved, some not.

Highlights: Here you'll find a vast variety of wineries to visit and wines to sample; assorted other row crops and orchards to view; hundreds of roadside fruit and vegetable stands to sample; funky themed towns, many restaurants and cafes, and accommodations ranging from RV parks to rustic B&Bs to four-star hotels at the end of the day.

It wasn't very long ago that the valley along the Yakima River from Selah to the Tri-Cities of Richland, Pasco, and Kennewick was barren of grapevines, except perhaps a few in private backyards. The Yakima Valley was best known for its commercial orchards, which grow apples, peaches, pears, cherries, apricots, and many other kinds of fruit. In the days BW (Before Wine), the valley wasn't a particularly inviting place because it was so hot and dusty and dry in the summer months, and cold and barren

Although grapes and wine have become synonymous with the Yakima Valley, apples—winesaps in this case—are still very important to the area. Asahel Curtis, Washington Historical Society

in the winter. But that has changed and wine shares the stage with fruit and vegetables. In fact, fruit growing is so important to the valley's economy and culture that the local chamber of commerce publishes a list of when food plants are ripe. The list contains more than 40 kinds of fruit and vegetables; any fruit that likes long, hot summers and can tolerate cold and dark winters is grown in the valley.

While all these fruits and vegetables are still grown in the valley, for the past several years they have been competing with grapevines, which now cover thousands of acres and are still spreading. Barns and silos have been replaced by new buildings with Old World charm in their architecture, and inside these buildings are enormous vats filled with fermenting grapes, and stacks and stacks of wooden barrels, all filled with the result of that fermentation: wine, thousands of oak barrels and enormous steel vats of red, white and some rosé wine. Wine has come to the valley and is here to stay.

Over the years the valley has been partitioned off into four American Viticultural Areas (AVAs), called appellations. This method of identifying wine growing areas is a convenient way to divide a large growing area, as is the Yakima Valley. It doesn't necessarily always make a lot of sense but since it has little or no effect on consumers and travelers, nobody cares. You can be grateful the French concept of terror has not yet taken hold in the American wine industry. Now there's a complicated concept. Following is one definition of AVAs so that you'll know the basics: An AVA specifies the geographical area where at least 85 percent of the grapes are grown that are used in making wine within the AVA. The designation has no effect on the types of grapes grown, nor does it reflect crop yields. The identification is sometimes confusing because, for example, the Columbia Valley appellation covers the Red Mountain, Yakima Valley, Walla Walla, Horse Heaven Hills, and Wahluke Slope appellations. So there are appellations inside appellations, something on the order of Russian nesting dolls.

Got that? Moving along swiftly—before someone asks the author a question because he is somewhat mystified by the overlapping—according to the Washington Wine Institute, Washington has nine American Viticultural Areas. The main AVAs you'll find on this trip are:

The Yakima Valley AVA was the first American Viticultural Area established in Washington (1983). Part of the larger Columbia Valley AVA, the Yakima Valley AVA is home to more than 11,000 acres of vineyards, giving the area the largest concentration of wineries and vineyards in the state of Washington. The most widely planted varietals in the area are Cabernet Sauvignon, Merlot, Syrah, Chardonnay, and Riesling. Nearly 40 percent of Washington state's yearly wine production is made from Yakima Valley grapes.

Snipes Mountain, which covers 4,145 acres between the towns of Sunnyside and Granger (around Outlook) in the southeast corner of the Yakima Valley, is a sub-AVA of the Yakima Valley and Columbia Valley AVAs. The Red Mountain AVA includes the land surrounding Red Mountain in Benton County. It is part of the Yakima Valley AVA, which in turn is part of the larger Columbia Valley AVA. Located between Benton City and Richland, the Red Mountain AVA is the smallest in the state, with only 4,040 acres. The area has 600 acres of primarily red varietals under culti-

Vineyards gracefully follow the contour of the land. Greater Yakima Valley Chamber of Commerce

vation, including Cabernet Sauvignon, Merlot, Sangiovese, Cabernet Franc, and Syrah.

The Wahluke Slope AVA is located in Grant County and it extends from the Columbia River in the west, the Hanford Site boundary in the southwest, the north bank of the Columbia River on the south up to the Wahluke Slope Wildlife Refuge in the east, and along the 1,480-foot elevation of the Saddle Mountain to the north. This area has the warmest grape-growing climate in the state. Three varieties of wine are most popular here: Cabernet Sauvignon, Merlot, and Syrah.

Understand? Good, let's hit the road.

Most visitors come to the Yakima Valley from the heavily populated Puget Sound basin, and they are lucky because arrival from the west is quite dramatic. First you go over Snoqualmie Pass on Interstate 5, and then you make the long ascent on sweeping curves through gradually thinning timber until you are in the open, windswept countryside. In this area most trees have a permanent eastward tilt because of the strong prevailing western winds that sweep down off the Cascades. Just beyond Ellensburg you take Interstate 82 southward and very soon begin a steep climb up the barren hills to the broad **Manastash Ridge Viewpoint.** From here you can see the breadth of the Yakima Valley spread out before you several miles ahead.

When you reach the valley floor on the banks of the **Yakima River,** you're immediately in the midst of vineyards and large roadside fruit and vegetable stands, and always a short distance off the Interstate are enticing restaurants and tempting hotels. During the busy summer season it is wise to book rooms before you leave home rather than searching for that perfect winery, then realizing as darkness falls that you may not find a place to sleep in the valley.

You can easily spend a day wandering around the town of **Yakima,** with its trendy shops, art galleries, restaurants, museums, wineries, and breweries. Many of these places are along the main drag, Yakima Avenue, which also hosts a farmer's market every Sunday from May through October. Another prime visitor area is the Historic District along North Front Street, where you'll find more restaurant, cafes, shops, and wine bars.

Mostly, though, it is the wine that brings visitors to the valley. Unless you know of specific wines and want to taste where they are made, or you have a list of wineries to visit, you might consider just ambling down the valley with a map from the chamber of commerce. All wineries have visiting hours posted and published, and all are easy to find. The three highways that run down the valley are in good condition, as are most county roads. But occasionally you will find a winery on a road that begins as blacktop and suddenly becomes washboardlike gravel and fine dirt. This dirt, mixed with volcanic ash from the Mount St. Helens eruption in 1980, leaves giant rooster tails of dust behind anything that moves—and it seeps into vehicles, so don't be surprised if you find a coating of powdery dust in the trunk of your car.

If you plan to taste wine at several wineries, it is wise to select someone in your party as the designated driver. As the chamber of commerce reminds visitors, "Wineries pour small tastes, but they add up." The alternative is to spit the wine into an elegant bucket that wineries keep handy for that purpose, much like spittoons in old-fashioned saloons. It may not be dainty, but spitting keeps you sober. Shall we move on to another subject?

While in Yakima you should stop in the **visitor information center** at 10 North 8th Street. Here you can pick up brochures and booklets that tell you about each winery, so you can make selections from these recommendations. Better yet, you can do your own version of a blind tasting by showing up at wineries without knowing anything about them other than their names; many visitors, especially those who do not need to impress anyone with their knowledge of wine, favor this approach. If for some obscure reason you won't be visiting wineries at all, you can still stop into the visitor center to buy some local wine.

Nearly all of the wineries are on the east side of the highways, and they become numerous about five miles southeast of the center of Yakima after Exit 40 on Interstate 82. This puts you on the northern edge of the Rattlesnake Hills appellation, and you will have more than twenty wineries from which to choose. One suggestion from the Yakima Valley Visitors and Convention Bureau on visiting the area: Since there are so many wineries, you might consider deciding in advance if you want to visit wineries out amid the vines, or if you prefer visiting tasting rooms in town. Or you can mix your winery visits with touring the small towns in the valley. One town in particular, **Prosser,** has a cluster of nearly two dozen wineries elbow-to-elbow in only two blocks. Several of the towns are worth at least a brief stop, and some have worked very hard at attracting tourists. You can visit wineries between the towns, dawdling and backtracking. This is a place where you should learn from small boys and happy dogs: Stop here, backtrack to see something again, zigzag without embarrassment, even stop and scratch if you feel the urge.

Since there are obviously too many wineries in the Yakima Valley to describe separately, you might begin your trek by visiting wineries in the towns and sampling their wines before heading to the vineyards. The **Tasting Room Yakima,** a cooperative that represents three wineries at 250 Ehler Road, is a good place to start. The **Barrel House** at 22 North First Street serves meals and has an extensive Washington wine list. The Barrel House has an unusual way of introducing Yakima Valley wines to newcomers: Their placemats have three circles, and a two-ounce glass of wine is placed on each circle. Two of the wines are from elsewhere, California and Australia, for example. The third circle is for a Yakima Valley wine so you can compare the three. Needless to say, the point they want to make is that Yakima Valley wines are just as good, and sometimes better.

Here is a sampling of winery towns. Heading south from Yakima, you'll go only four or five miles before reaching **Union Gap,** which is mostly a working town with the usual selection of fast food outlets. It has a few lovely old gingerbread-style houses, and also has the **Central Washington Agricultural Museum** on the south end of town, just off WA 97 in Fullbright Park.

Wapato is interesting for its dominant Hispanic population, which a recent estimate put at 85 percent. Today everyone, Hispanics and Anglos, refers to Wapato as a Mexican town, but it has always been home to ethnic groups other than Anglo. Around the turn of the twentieth century Wapato attracted many people of Japanese descent from Hawaii; one particular area was called Japanese Town, and its Japanese American population rivaled that of Seattle. The first Buddhist church in Washington was built in Wapato and opened in 1936. Sadly, it closed in 1941 and was destroyed during the panic that followed the Japanese attack on Pearl Harbor in December 1941. President Roosevelt signed the misguided Executive Order 9066, which forced all persons of Japanese descent to evacuate Wapato and be taken to internment camps further inland. Then, during World War II, German prisoners of war held in a camp outside town were pressed into duty caring for the orchards and fields. A few Japanese Americans were being held in nearby internment camps, and they were also taken to the fields and orchards. At the end of the war, a labor shortage created a void that was filled by Hispanic migrant workers, and the Bracero Program, the

This gigantic teapot once was a service station but it has been turned into a beloved Yakima Valley landmark. Greater Yakima Valley Chamber of Commerce

guest-worker program agreed to by the United States and Mexico during the war.

Zillah is next, a small, pleasant town named for a crying child. Zillah Oakes was the daughter of Thomas Fletcher Oakes, who as president of the Northern Pacific Railway had backed the building of the Sunnyside Canal. Zillah cried and screamed all the way to the new town. Her father promised to name the town after her if she would stop. It apparently worked.

Another mild oddity of Zillah is the name of the conservative Church of God, officially the Church of God Zillah. Some in the congregation were not amused by this nomenclatural accident, but the majority decided to join the fun and erected a wire-frame Godzilla float outside the church.

On the heels of a major 1920s political scandal involving the oil business, the Teapot Dome, someone in the next town, Toppenish, had an ambitious idea: He would build a gas station in the shape of a teapot to make his statement about the scandal. The deed was done. The Teapot Dome Service Station was built in 1922 on US 12. The round building has a conical roof, sheet metal "handle," and a concrete "spout." The unique service station continued operation as a full service gas station for some years. When Interstate 82 was constructed near Zillah, the station was relocated less than a mile down the Yakima Valley Highway. Sadly, it is no longer in operation but it is on the National Register of Historic Places and is a favorite with photographers.

Toppenish is the next town and, in at least one way, the most spectacular. A town that bridges the cultural gap between the Anglos, Hispanics, the peoples of the Yakima Indian Reservation, and a few other cultures, Toppenish celebrates this diversity with murals. These are enormous murals that cover entire walls of buildings downtown. So far the total is around 70 murals, and new ones are added each year. The murals have a definite Old West theme, with Indians, cowboys, and stagecoaches galore, plus a few more contemporary scenes. You can tour the murals in a covered horse-drawn wagon. An annual event that attracts artists, critics, and photographers from all over the Northwest is the Mural-in-A-Day held the first Saturday of June. Numerous artists clamber around a wall, many on ladders, to complete a mural before sunset. It is one of the most popular events in the Yakima Valley.

South of Toppenish the wineries thin out until you reach Prosser, about 25 miles later. Here you'll find a cluster of around two dozen wineries in

Toppenish is one of the best-known mural towns in the Northwest. Greater Yakima Valley Chamber of Commerce

about two blocks, along with gourmet foods sold in tasting rooms. Some wineries serve appetizers every day, others only on weekends throughout the summer

Another 20 miles brings you to Benton City, which is surrounded by about a dozen wineries. Benton City is on the western edge of the Tri-Cities and its half-dozen wineries. With a combined population of 230,000, the Tri-Cities are Washington's fourth largest city, to the point where it is virtually impossible to differentiate between the three. You will find all the amenities of large cities here, four-star hotels, excellent restaurants, shopping . . . the works.

If this route sounds too tame for you by hugging the main highways, you might consider this alternative. While still in Yakima, watch for WA 24 west, which is Exit 34 off I-82. Almost immediately you will be surrounded by hops orchards, which at first glance look much like very tall grapevines because they grow up to fourteen feet high on trellises. Grapes are big in the Yakima Valley, but hop growing is bigger on a national basis: something like 75 percent of all hops grown in the U.S. are grown in the Yakima Valley. Take South Faucher Road south off Highway 20, which soon connects to Konnowac Pass Road. Take that winding road south over the low pass and you are in the heart of the Rattlesnake Hills wine district. Be sure and have a map of the vineyards with you because this route leads to many wineries. It soon connects with the main highways along the Yakima River.

IN THE AREA

Accommodations

Birchfield Manor Country Inn, 2018 Burchfield Rd., Yakima. Call 1-800-375-3420 or 509-452-1960. For more than 30 years the Burchfield has been either the best inn and restaurant in the valley, or at least one of the two or three best. The original manor house has five rooms above the restaurant, and the newer addition has six more rooms. Prices begin around $120 a night. Dinners are quite expensive, but the food is renowned throughout the Northwest. In addition to breakfast and dinner (lunch is not served), the inn offers casual poolside dining with tapas, specialty pizzas, and assorted small plates, plus wine from a different winery each week. Poolside snacks begin at $7.50 each, and wine is $8 a glass. Live music completes the affair.

Outlook Inn Guest House, Tefft Cellars Winery, 1320 Independence Rd., Outlook. Call 1-888-549-7244. Outlook is a very small town on WA 12 between Granger and Sunnyside, and Tefft Cellars is a short distance east of Outlook on the southern edge of the Rattlesnake Hills appellation. This guest house features three guest rooms with queen beds and full baths with showers. The kitchen is fully equipped. There's a large, secluded deck overlooking the vineyards on the back of the house. Rentals have a two-night minimum at $395 for two nights, plus damage and pet deposits.

The Vintner's Inn at Hinzerling Winery, 1520 Sheridan Ave., Prosser. Call 1-800-727-6702 or 509-786-2163. The Hinzerling Winery, owned by

Jerry Wallace and his son Mike, is believed to be the oldest family-owned and -operated winery in the Yakima Valley, dating back to 1976. In 2001 the Wallaces opened the two-bedroom Vintner's Inn in a 1905 farmhouse next door to their winery. Many of the original features and fixtures remain, including claw-foot bathtubs with hand-held showerheads (rather than standup showers). In what neighbors and friends say is Jerry's typical approach to things, here is how their brochure handles the problem of noise: "We are located in the center of Prosser about three blocks from the railroad tracks—if the passing of trains or an occasional potato truck during the night would disturb you or interfere with your rest, you may wish other accommodations." Rates begin at $89 for the main room; the smaller room is less. The bathroom is shared.

Attractions and Recreation

Barrel House, 22 N. First St., Yakima. Call 509-453-3769.

Central Washington Agricultural Museum, 4508 Main St., Union Gap, Phone 509-457-8735 or 248-0432.

Tasting Room Yakima, 250 Ehler Rd., Yakima. Call 509-966-0686.

Other Contacts

Yakima Valley Visitor Information Center, 101 North Fair Ave., Yakima. Call 509-573-3388 or 800-221-0751. Web site: www.visityakima.com

Saddle Mountain looms over the Crab Creek Valley just before the state's longest creek empties into the Columbia River.

CHAPTER

13

The Best of the Crab Creek Valley

Estimated length: About 20 miles
Estimated time: 1 hour

Getting there: From WA 243 in Beverly, go east on this gravel-and-dirt road until it joins WA 26 near Royal City.

Highlights: You will follow a meandering stream past sand dunes and small lakes, all in the looming presence of Saddle Mountain.

Crab Creek is believed to be the longest creek in Washington, and is the only year-around creek in the Channeled Scablands. It is born a short distance west of Spokane and meanders west across the wheat country to Odessa, then gets involved with the Columbia Basin Project as one of the streams that help drain water that has been used for irrigation. It heads south, more or less, from the Soap Lake area, enters Moses Lake and temporarily loses itself in the lake, then reemerges below the Potholes Reservoir with its own identity again. Soon it heads due west along the base of the Saddle Mountains, and finally enters the Columbia River just downstream from the very small town of Beverly.

Some geography students like to follow the creek from its source to the Columbia, but that is too complicated for this book. Instead, we will concentrate on the last stretch before it reaches the Columbia, where the creek wanders along the base of the mountains and is paralleled by a modest road before losing itself by emptying into the Columbia.

Going off in search of Crab Creek's modest estuary gives you a good excuse, or reason, to stop at the **Ginkgo Petrified Forest State Park/ Wanapum Recreational Area** at Vantage, a 7,470-acre park including 27,000 feet of shoreline on the Columbia River. Be warned: If you visit Vantage in July or August, you might as well be in Twentynine Palms, California, because the temperature can soar to more than 110 degrees Fahrenheit down in the Columbia River canyon. However, the state park is worth the sunburn because it has the best collection of petrified wood in the state: More than 200 species of petrified wood have been identified here, including the ginkgo, which is otherwise extinct in America. The park includes a museum and an interpretive trail.

From Vantage, go east across the Columbia River and turn south immediately after crossing the bridge. Take State 26 until the intersection with the more modest State 243, and take it south along the river to Beverly.

It was at this intersection that my son and I once had a strange adventure. We were coming up from Beverly and were waiting at the State 243–State 26 junction for trucks to pass when a semi loaded with hay came roaring down the hill. When it turned south on the sharp curve there, a whole section of baled hay flew off and scattered along the road like scraps of paper.

I parked, and my son and I ran over to pull the hay off the road before someone hit it with a car. Another car stopped and the driver got out to help, and another truck loaded with hay stopped. He radioed ahead to tell the first trucker he had lost part of his load. Only after we had dragged several bales off the highway did I see a man sitting on a bale in the ditch, holding his head. I said what everyone says in such a situation: "Are you all right?"

He didn't answer for a moment. He was covered with hay and dirt, and his right hand was skinned. He didn't have any teeth, and he hadn't shaved in a few days.

"I think so," he finally said. "I'll be all right in a minute." Then he started talking and was still talking when we drove away several minutes later. "I was just walking along when he dumped his load on me," he said. Neither my son nor I saw him beside the road when we were waiting for traffic to clear.

"Knocked my feet right out from under me. My cigarette lighter is lay-ing way over there," he said, pointing toward the ditch. My son, the truck driver, and I all stopped working and stood around listening to his story. "I was just walking along when, boom! he got me. I ran out of gas up at Moses Lake and was walking down here, where I've got a cache of gas behind a pile of rocks."

Then he lost all of us. Moses Lake is about 40 miles away, on another highway, and none of us believed him. He kept talking, elaborating his story and trying to sound put-upon for being such an innocent victim. We decided that he had hidden between the stacks of baled hay to hitch a ride, but had loosened them so much that they flew off on the first turn. He was still talking when we left. I have always wondered if the gods of cir-cumstance weren't feeling a little petulant that day.

Although I'm personally not fond of dams (even though I am using electricity from them at this very moment), you may want to stop at the **Wanapum Dam** because it has a good regional museum that emphasizes Native American culture, and a viewing window where you can watch salmon and other fish using the ladder around the dam.

The Crab Creek route begins in Beverly, a small, sun-baked town over-looking the Columbia. It is worth noting that the Columbia River from Wanapum Dam downriver through the Hanford Nuclear Reservation is the only stretch of the Columbia within the United States that still flows unin-hibited by dams. It isn't a long stretch—only about 60 miles—and its vol-ume is controlled by dams upstream. At least the water moves, giving you a sense of what it was like before the arrival of dams and the hydroelec-tric-hungry aluminum plants the dams brought to the riverbanks. These facilities were built in the days before power brokers even thought of com-paring the number of jobs created against the cost to the fishing industry and Native American culture.

All along the lower Crab Creek valley, **Saddle Mountain** looms over the eastern bank, casting long shadows in the morning and showing various colors in the evening. Some of the mountain is smooth, and looks as though you could hike to the top in an hour or so. In other places it is a sheer cliff, with wind-carved hoodoos creating almost as many forms as a summer cloud. The valley is particularly pretty in the spring, when all plants are green and desert wildflowers bloom on the valley floor and up the sides of Saddle Mountain.

Part of the valley's extensive sand dunes have been designated a play-

It is very hard to drive through Eastern Washington in the summer without stopping frequently for fruit, berries and produce, all grown within sight of the fruit stand.

ground for all-terrain vehicles. The rest of the valley is divided among farming, grazing, the wetlands of the **Crab Creek Wildlife Area,** and parts of the **Columbia National Wildlife Refuge.** Here you'll see birds in the marsh grass year-round, ranging from migratory waterfowl to small songbirds. Lakes spot the valley. Some of the lakes have bans on motors, so fishermen must hike in with their equipment. Since Crab Creek is part of the Columbia Basin's drainage system, its water is rich with nutrients. Rainbow and eastern brook trout grow to larger-than-usual sizes here.

Most of the road through the valley is dirt and gravel, the kind that forces you to drive slower than usual so you can savor the quiet beauty of the place. You will go through the remnants of three towns that thrived briefly in the valley. The valley was settled when the Milwaukee Railroad was built long after the major railroads reached the West Coast. The Milwaukee line didn't have the advantage of free land that was given to the other railroads, the Great Northern and Union Pacific, so it had to buy track right-of-way in more hostile and less populated areas. In the Crab Creek valley at least three sidings were built: in Smyrna, Corfu, and Taunton. Today only a suggestion remains of each. The last time I drove through the valley, the schoolhouse in Smyrna had been converted into a home.

The Milwaukee Railroad went out of business many years ago and the state of Washington acquired the track bed for use as a cross-state hiking, horseback, and bicycle trail, parts of which were named in honor of the patriotic actor John Wayne.

The route ends when the road intersects with State 26 a few miles west of Othello.

IN THE AREA

Attractions and Recreation

Columbia National Wildlife Refuge, 735 E Main St., Othello. Call 509-488-2668.

Gingko Petrified Forest State Park/Wanapum Recreational Area, 4571 Huntzinger Rd., Vantage. Call 509-856-2700.

The sky seems larger in Eastern Washington, and the rain clouds are often more dramatic than the dense clouds along the coast and Puget Sound.

14

Down the Columbia to the Sea

Estimated length: 70 miles
Estimated time: 2–3 hours

Getting there: Take WA 4 from I-5 at Kelso and follow it until you reach WA 403 for the side trip to Altoona. Return to WA 4 and continue west to WA 401. Take WA 401 south to Megler, the Astoria Bridge, and the Long Beach Peninsula.

Highlights: This route follows the broad Columbia River with its ocean-going traffic, sloughs with anchored log booms, the Julia Butler Hansen National Wildlife Refuge featuring the white-tailed deer, picturesque river towns, the Long Beach Peninsula, and the Pacific Ocean.

Locally this is called the Ocean Beach Highway for the simple and obvious reason that it is the route people in the Longview–Kelso area take to the Long Beach Peninsula. It is a beautiful highway and does not seem to have even one dull mile, although services are limited.

The Columbia River is almost an arm of the Pacific Ocean because it is so subject to the ebb and flow of the tides. This effect can be seen and felt all the way upstream to the Bonneville Dam in the Columbia Gorge. This tidal flow is so strong that tug boats towing barges or log booms must move with the tide because a heavily loaded tug sometimes cannot move at all against the tide. So the skippers have learned to either tie up to shore, or to loiter in coves and sloughs and wait until the tide reaches its peak and stops running. Another alternative is to time their trips to coincide with the tidal flow going in their direction.

The Columbia is dredged regularly to keep a channel deep enough for oceangoing ships, and this gives the river a maritime look. It can be disconcerting when you are driving along the highway and suddenly see an enormous ship only a few feet away from you, looking as incongruous as an elephant down by the old mill stream.

The highway follows the river closely for the first several miles and doesn't really leave it until it reaches the county line between Cowlitz and Wahkiakum counties. Here a long beach has been developed by dredge spoils, which is the sand and dirt pumped ashore from the dredges. The beach is popular with fishermen who cast their lures far out into the river, then attach their rods to various clamps and racks. They attach a bell or other signaling device to the tip of the rod and then go about their social life, one ear always cocked for the bell while they visit, drink coffee, stoke

Skamokawa Creek serves as a parking lot for many commercial fishing boats.

the beach fire or watch television in their RV. Because these fishing spots are so popular with retired people, many share the generic nickname Social Security Beach.

The first town of any size after leaving Longview is **Cathlamet,** the county seat of Wahkiakum County. It is one of the oldest towns on the Columbia River and was founded by a former Hudson's Bay employee named Birnie. He befriended several American soldiers stationed upriver at Vancouver Barracks, which replaced Fort Vancouver when the international boundary between Canada and the United States was established. Among those soldiers was a lonely lieutenant with a drinking problem named Ulysses S. Grant, who made several trips downriver to visit Birnie.

Cathlamet has remained genuinely historical, with several of the old homes and business buildings restored and occupied by hotels, B&Bs, and restaurants. The town was built on a hilly piece of land overlooking **Puget Island,** the only inhabited island in the Columbia River. While most Cathlamet residents are descendants of Scandinavian and Finnish immigrants, many Puget Island residents are second- and third-generation immigrants from Switzerland. Its industry is about evenly divided between dairy farming and commercial fishing, with boatbuilding thrown in.

The island is laced by several canals where commercial fishing boats are moored. It is connected to Cathlamet by a bridge, and to Oregon by a small car ferry. This is the only place the Columbia can be crossed between the bridge at Longview and the four-mile-long Astoria-Megler Bridge.

Just downstream from Cathlamet you will enter the **Julia Butler Hansen National Wildlife Refuge.** Originally it was named for the Columbian white-tailed deer, an endangered subspecies of their larger white-tailed cousins now found only on this refuge and some of the islands in the river. WA 4 goes along the edge of the refuge, but for the best views of the small deer and the birds that frequent the refuge, turn off the main highway at the refuge entrance and drive along a dike road through the refuge. The road rejoins WA 4 at the town of Skamokawa.

Skamokawa is one of the more picturesque of the Columbia River towns. It was built where Skamokawa Creek empties into the Columbia and served as a stop for river steamboats for many years. Its reportedly was a local Native American word meaning "smoke over the water," because fog frequently hangs over the creek that snakes down from the foothills through the valley.

The most familiar building in Skamokawa is the Redmen Hall, built

This Skamokawa landmark was once home to a social club, but the club disappeared, leaving this striking building.

several feet above the highway on a hillside at the east end of the bridge. The Redmen was a fraternal organization of several decades ago that gradually disappeared, leaving the striking building behind. It has since been taken over by the town as a community center and museum.

After Skamokawa the highway swings away from the river and goes back into the forest, climbs over the low summit of KM Mountain and drops back down to the Grays River Valley. The town of Grays River was built at the crossing of the small, flat river that meanders through the pastureland. The town of Grays River once had a dairy cooperative processing plant and a general store, but it dwindled steadily until almost nothing is left. It undoubtedly will follow the pattern of other towns in Washington that have faded, then returned to life in another form.

Only a short distance west of town is the **Grays River Covered Bridge,** standing alone in the pastureland below the highway. It is the only covered bridge still in use in Washington, and its weight load has diminished to the point that trucks can't use it. Local history buffs keep it in working order.

At the one- or two-building town of Rosburg, treat yourself to a pleasant few minutes by taking WA 405 south to the Columbia River. The blacktop road twists and turns its way along the edge of the low hills, following

For many years the Grays River Covered Bridge has stood out in this pasture, seldom used but protected so that it will remain as a landmark.

the Grays River into Grays Bay, a broad arm of the Columbia River. The road goes along the east side of the bay to the Columbia River, then takes a sharp left turn up the Columbia River to Conttardi, Altoona, and Pillar Rock, which is about four miles further on a dirt road. These towns began as large salmon canneries built on stilts above the river so that fishing boats could offload directly onto the cannery floors. They also built stores on the stilts, and small houses for workers were built on the narrow shelf of land beneath the bluffs, barely leaving room for a road to go between the river and the houses. Little is left of the towns today because they gradually rot away and fall into the river, but enough remains to get an idea of what once was a major industry.

After returning to the main route, you will go through more forest and along the Naselle River until you come to the town of Naselle. Here you can follow WA 4 to its intersection with US 101 beside Willapa Bay, or turn south in Naselle on WA 401, which leads back down to the Columbia River, the Astoria–Megler Bridge, and around the giant estuary to Chinook, Ilwaco, and the Long Beach Peninsula.

IN THE AREA

Attractions and Recreation

Julia Butler Hansen National Wildlife Refuge, 46 Steamboat Slough Rd., Cathlamet. Call 360-795-3915.

15

Through the Heart of Lewis County

Estimated length: 55 miles
Estimated time: 2 hours

Getting there: From I-5 in Chehalis, take Exit 77 and follow WA 6 a short distance to WA 603, which takes you to Vader. Turn west on WA 506 to Ryderwood turnoff. Return to 506 and take it to Pe Ell, where you will take WA 6 to Raymond.

Highlights: This route passes bucolic rural scenery, small towns filled with fans of high school football, a town with all residents above retirement age, and Washington's smallest state park.

This is the kind of countryside where you'll see the names of the local high school teams proudly displayed in the towns and on car bumpers. Although the larger towns, such as Chehalis, are steadily growing and creating suburbs far out into the countryside, this area retains its bucolic atmosphere. While this route won't offer you gourmet food or elaborate places to sleep, it is a very pleasant antidote to freeways, cutesy cafes and expensive restaurants. Take your time. It is countryside travel at its best.

Start this loop trip from Interstate 5 at Chehalis. Take Exit 77 and drive west on State 6 a short distance to State 603, which heads south to Napavine, Winlock, and Vader. Most of the scenery to Napavine is given over to newer homes built along the highway, but occasionally on clear days you can see Mount Rainier and Mount St. Helens. Once you reach **Napavine,** the houses thin out and the scenery becomes more rural, with lots of dairy cattle munching back and forth across the low hills in meadows cleared from fir and hemlock forest.

In the middle of **Winlock** you will see an enormous egg with a sign proclaiming it the biggest egg in the world. It would be a scary event indeed to meet a bird that could lay one that large. Fear not: It is made of reinforced concrete. It is there because, while the main north–south highway, US 99, was being built in the 1920s, all towns between Seattle and Portland were asked to participate in the opening celebration with a float. In those days of few automobiles highway construction was a big news event, unlike today when traffic is so heavy that when construction workers take down the barricades they must run for their lives. Winlock was in the egg business in a big way then, so the town created a gigantic papier-mâché egg to put on a float. Since it made a big hit in the parade, a collection was taken up to build an even larger egg, this one of concrete, and it was placed on wooden poles with a sign proclaiming Winlock the Egg Capital of the World.

Winlock is very proud of this egg.
Winlock Chamber of Commerce

Some years later, as if the Humpty Dumpty story had to be authenticated, the poles rotted and collapsed, dropping the egg to the ground and smashing it into many pieces. By this time Winlock was no longer noted in the egg business but the egg was too much a part of the town's identity, so another collection was taken and the townsfolk built another egg, of durable plastic this time, and placed it on a pedestal near the railroad.

The next town is Vader, a very small town with one of those many disputes over nomenclature as part of its heritage. It began its life as Little

NOMENCLATURE

Charles Nordoff, a nineteenth-century journalist and author, visited Washington Territory in 1874 after touring the Hawaiian Islands (then called the Sandwich Islands) and California. He liked most things about Washington, but he did not like Washington's choice of place names. In his book *Northern California, Oregon, and the Sandwich Islands,* he explained why:

When, at Kalama, you enter Washington Territory, your ears begin to be assailed by the most barbarous names imaginable. On your way to Olympia by rail you cross a river called Skookum-Chuck; your train stops at places named Newaukum, Tumwater, and Toutle; and if you seek further, you will hear of whole counties labeled Wahkiakum, or Snohomish, or Kitsap, or Klikatat; and Cowlitz, Hookium, and Nenolelops greet and offend you. They complain in Olympia that Washington Territory gets but little immigration; but what wonder? What man, having the whole American continent to chose from, would willingly date his letters from the county of Snohomish, or bring up his children in the city of Nenolelops? The village of Tumwater is, as I am ready to bear witness, very pretty indeed; but surely an emigrant would think twice before he established himself either there or at Toutle. Seattle is sufficiently barbarous; Steilacoom is no better; and I suspect that the Northern Pacific Railroad terminus has been fixed at Tacoma—if it is fixed there—because that is one of the few places on Puget Sound whose name does not inspire horror and disgust.

Falls, but the Northern Pacific Railroad folks pointed out they already had a Little Falls on their line, so the local folks, which undoubtedly included a former Canadian or two, wanted to name it Toronto. After the usual argument, the namers finally agreed to name it for a German resident named Vader. Why he was so honored was not recorded. The name became formal and Mr. Vader, for unrecorded reasons, immediately packed his stuff and moved to Florida, never to return.

Several years ago, when I first drove this road, I was pleasantly surprised to see that someone had placed a set of signs along the road in honor of the old **Burma-Shave signs.** In case you are too young to have ever seen those signs, they were stationed along America's highways for nearly 40 years; the first went up in 1925 and the last in 1963. Most consisted of five lines, with the fifth line always reading "BURMA-SHAVE." It was a minor thrill to see the reincarnated Burma-Shave signs near Vader that read:

THEY MISSED THE TURN

CAR WAS WHIZZ'N

FAULT WAS HER'N

FUNERAL HIS'N

BURMA-SHAVE

I took out one of my favorite books, *Verse by the Side of the Road,* by Frank Rowsome, and went through it again to read my favorites, suffering a serious attack of nostalgia for the days when I owned a canary-yellow 1946 Ford convertible and waited anxiously for the next set of Burma-Shave signs.

These are some of my favorites:

SLOW DOWN PA

SAKES ALIVE

MA MISSED SIGNS

FOUR AND FIVE

SHE KISSED THE HAIRBRUSH

BY MISTAKE

SHE THOUGHT IT WAS

HER HUSBAND JAKE

IF YOU THINK

SHE LIKES YOUR BRISTLES

WALK BARE-FOOTED

THROUGH SOME THISTLES

THIRTY DAYS

HATH SEPTEMBER

APRIL, JUNE, AND THE

SPEED OFFENDER

The resurrected Burma-Shave signs put me in the proper frame of mind for the small town of **Ryderwood,** at the end of a dead-end spur off WA 536. Seventy-some years ago, when the Long-Bell Lumber Company came to Washington from the Carolinas and went into the business of cutting trees in the area and sawing them into logs and boards, the company

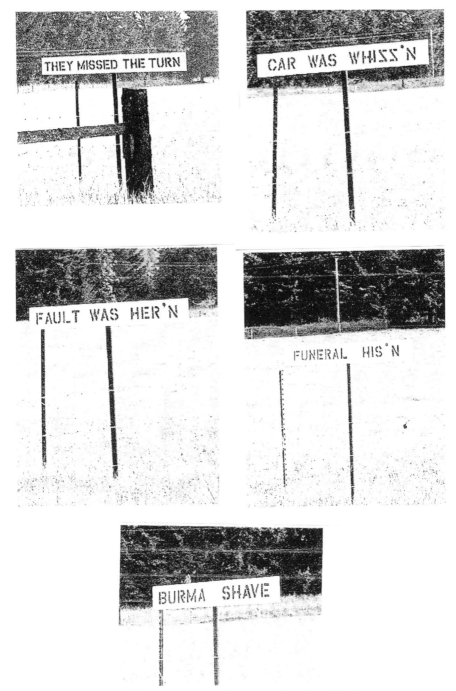

This series of signs celebrating Burma Shave was found on WA 6.

had to build its own towns here and there for its employees. Ryderwood was one of them. When Long-Bell went out of business, some of the towns remained and some were abandoned. Ryderwood was one that stayed alive, and it did so by becoming a retirement village.

The village came into being in 1923 and for a while proudly proclaimed itself the "World's Largest Logging Camp." It was one of the very few logging camps that was built so that families could live there rather than single men only. This was in part a result of the generosity of spirit shown by the Long-Bell founder, Robert Alexander Long, whose personal motto was "Be of service, even it is necessary to go out of your way." It was a motto he lived up to at the small town of Ryderwood, and the much larger and more important town of Longview, not far away at the conjunction of the Cowlitz and Columbia Rivers. By the early 1950s all the trees worth cutting were gone and only stumps, piles of branches and dead trees littered the mountains around Ryderwood. Since it normally took around 40 years for new trees to become large enough to cut, Long-Bell abandoned the area to wait for the new forest to grow. But Robert A. Long kind of liked Ryderwood and would not permit his employees to raze the town. In the meantime, the population shrank from a high of around two thousand to fewer than one hundred. In 1953 the company set aside 130,000 acres as a tree farm and put the town up for sale.

That fall, a Los Angeles real-estate developer named Harry Kem came for a look, liked what he saw, and decided to buy the entire town and use it to put one of his dream projects into effect. He knew that many retirees had a hard time finding affordable places to live, so he and some friends bought Ryderwood from Long-Bell for $90,000. Then Kem send in crews to fix up 205 of the town's 400 houses, and tore down those beyond hope. Once the houses were rehabilitated, Kem offered them for sale. The 150 two-bedroom houses listed at $2,500 each—$200 down and $20 a month—and the 55 three-bedroom houses were $3,500 at $3,500 down and $30 a month. Buyers were restricted to retired people with income of at least $135 a month and no more than $250. Ten acres were set aside as a communal garden, the town's recreational hall was refurbished, and an eight-bed hospital was built with medical care insurance costing $2 a month. Although Kem's plan was generous to the citizens, he of course was making money on the operation. He made no pretenses about the profit motive. He said that he and his partners might make $1 million in profit from the adventure.

The town is still going strong, although the hospital plan was abandoned several years ago. The main change in town has been the value of its properties. Those houses that sold for $2,500 to $3,500? Today, none can be bought for less than $100,000. It isn't at all inactive, though. I was once sent there by a newspaper for a story on the town and everyone was so busy with various projects and interests that we could hardly get anyone to talk to us. Our original plan was to line up everyone in town for a group photo, but that was totally out of the question. They just weren't interested, and most didn't care if their names and pictures were in the paper at all. It was an attitude I found refreshing after being pursued by people desperate for public attention. We got a story but it wasn't much, the editor told us.

With the memory of that event fresh in mind, when I last drove through Ryderwood, I did so only to refresh my visual memory, and as before, hardly anybody was on the street and no tricycles or other indications of young people was showing. I did see some people working in their gardens and on roofs, but I didn't see anyone sitting on the front porch doing nothing.

From Ryderwood the road becomes almost a boulevard between dairy farms, and nearly every farm I passed had some kind of dairy award noted or posted on the fences, by the mailboxes, or at the gates. Some of the houses and farm buildings are right beside the highway as though the farmers didn't want to waste good farmland on things like lawns, but I suspect that the buildings are in their original places and the highway widened.

At the small village of Boistfort the main road goes almost due north back to State 6, but the drive west on the smaller, quieter paved road to the town of **Pe Ell** is prettier. Pe Ell began life as Pierre, but local legend has it that the local Native Americans couldn't pronounce the R's in Pierre, saying something like "Pe Ell" instead, so the name stuck.

The next town has a similar story. The founder of Lebam had a daughter named Mabel. He reversed the spelling when it came time to name the town. We can only hope Mabel thought it was funny.

From Lebam it is an easy drive on in to Raymond and US 101, but you should make one more stop and pay homage to the man whose grave constitutes Washington's smallest state park. It is Willie Keil's Grave State Park about five miles east of Raymond.

It is a grave with a strange story. Willie Keil was the nineteen-year-old son of William Keil, a Prussian who came to America around 1800 as a tailor. This was the era of Christian communism, and all over Europe and

North America Christian and Utopian communes were formed, some quite successful. William Keil was the founder of a group that settled in Bethel, Missouri, a short distance west of Hannibal. The commune was successful and its members became very wealthy. When the Oregon fever struck America in the 1840s, the commune, by now called the Bethelites, was also afflicted with the fever, and the commune decided that a group of its members should go forth and start a new commune in the Oregon Country. Dr. William Keil decided to lead the group.

Young Willie was probably the most excited member of the party, but a short time before the expedition left he fell ill with malaria. As he lay dying, he hallucinated and sometimes believed he was at the head of the wagon train, leading the group across the plains and mountains. During his lucid moments, he pleaded with his parents to promise that he could go with them. Soon the boy died and the parents set about keeping their promise to him. They had a casket built with a lead lining and filled it with alcohol and placed the boy's body in it. They loaded the casket onto a wagon Keil had built especially to carry the ill boy. Now it was made into a hearse. All the way across the plains and mountains to the Oregon Country the hearse wagon led the party.

Word went ahead via the moccasin telegraph of the unusual procession, and they were left alone by the Indians who liked to prey on wagon trains. However, the Blackfeet tribe didn't know about the Bethelites and one night they stole some cattle from the procession. Before long the cattle were back; other tribes had told the Blackfeet about the hearse and that was enough to make the Blackfeet believe the travelers should be left alone.

When the group reached Willapa Bay they established a village and held a decent burial for Willie on a hillside five miles from Raymond with a view to the north. The Bethelites soon realized that they had not selected a good place for a town—too remote and too damp—so they packed up and moved to a site not far south of Portland. They named it Aurora in honor of the Keils' daughter and the town still stands—as does its sister town, Bethel, Missouri.

IN THE AREA

Accommodations

Lodging and dining in Lewis County are limited to inexpensive motels and country cafes.

A wave crashes against Cape Disappointment during one of the frequent storms that hit the coast here. Long Beach Chamber of Commerce

CHAPTER

16

Rounding the Peninsula on US 101

Estimated length: 375 miles
Estimated time: 3–5 days

Getting there: Join US 101 at the Astoria–Megler Bridge and stay on the highway all the way around the Olympic Peninsula.

Highlights: You'll see dramatic coastline scenery, beginning with the Long Beach Peninsula, and many stretches of unspoiled coast; some of the largest and oldest trees in America; casual and unpretentious small towns; Olympic National Park, which spans from coast to mountains; the Strait of Juan de Fuca (with Canada's Vancouver Island across the strait); and Hood Canal.

This is one of the most beautiful drives in the state, and for that matter in the country. Calling a major U.S. highway a backroad may be stretching the definition beyond the breaking point, but US 101 is the highway that takes you entirely around the Olympic Peninsula, and much of it feels and looks like a country road. The Olympic Peninsula is relatively undeveloped, thanks to the Olympic National Park, Olympic National Forest, and the Quinault, Makah, Shoalwater, and Quillayute Indian reservations. It also has some of the most rugged landscape and coastline you'll find in the country without going to Alaska.

If you think you can "do" the Olympic Peninsula in only two days, you'll be disappointed. Although it is only a bit more than 300 miles from the Columbia River around the Olympic Peninsula to the end of the highway near Olympia, you should allow yourself three days minimum. Otherwise you will be forced to eliminate some of the highlights, and no matter which ones you drop, you'll go home with regrets.

US 101 comes within fifty miles of making a complete loop during its three-hundred-plus-mile sojourn through Washington; that is the distance from Aberdeen, at the foot of the Olympic Peninsula, to the highway's terminus at Olympia. The route, traveling from south to north as described here, begins at the north side of the Columbia River at the Astoria–Megler toll bridge. From the bridge the highway runs northwest along the bank of the vast river estuary. Here it is so broad that it looks more like the open ocean than a river mouth.

Much of Fort Columbia was buried in a low headland, out of reach of enemy artillery. Now a state park, the fort began as an army base to protect the northern side of the entrance to the Columbia River. Like Fort Stevens, its counterpart on the Oregon side, Fort Columbia was equipped with cannons, called disappearing rifles (see chapter 4). The guns of Fort Columbia never fired a shot in anger and the fort was eventually abandoned and the lovely spot donated to the state. The park is small and modest and is greatly overshadowed by Fort Stevens across the river, which is much larger and is one of Oregon's most heavily used parks. Part of the reason Fort Columbia has such a low profile is the large number of other things to do, and other large parks in the immediate area have better views and beaches.

For several decades, the area from **Chinook to Ilwaco** was one of the richest commercial salmon-fishing areas in the world. Salmon came into the shallow waters on their way upriver to their spawning streams, and fishermen were waiting for them with long nets that were pulled out into the shallow water by horses. When a net was extended to its full length, the horses pulled each end to shore, bringing thousands of salmon and other fish onto dry land. Enormous salmon canneries were built here, in Astoria (across the river), and upstream at Knappton, Altoona, Pillar Rock, and other sites. The salmon were so thick that people honestly believed they could never all be caught, that they would keep coming back to the river forever, that they were a renewable resource, like rain, that needed no help to replenish itself. It didn't take long for many of the same people to predict

Ilwaco has some striking murals in its small downtown district.

an end to the salmon supply, but it did almost take too long for the government to do anything about it. Today the salmon is perhaps the world's most heavily subsidized creature.

During those years when horse-drawn nets were used, fishermen also built large traps along the shore to direct the homeward-bound fish into an enclosed area, where they could be bailed out into waiting boats. It has been said that at one time Chinook, Washington, was the wealthiest town in America on a per capita basis, but that changed when the salmon runs were found to be almost depleted and the large nets and fish traps were outlawed. Some fishermen still work out of Chinook and Ilwaco, but the industry is more a memory than a reality today. Commercial fishing boats now share the marinas with salmon charter boats.

Just outside Ilwaco is a cluster of attractions worth a detour. First is Fort Canby State Park, a large park with lots of room for camping. It also has some of the best beaches, walking trails, and viewpoints in the area.

On around the estuary a short distance, at the base of Cape Disappointment, is the U.S. Coast Guard's National Motor Lifeboat School. This is where the coxswains of those tough, fast surfboats are trained, and the site was selected because it has more days of rough water than anywhere else outside Alaska. The coxswains are trained to operate the lifeboats that are so strongly built that they can flip over in the surf, right themselves, and keep going. Crewmen are strapped on to these boats and veterans of overturns say it is incredibly noisy under water, and that although it usually takes less than thirty seconds for the boat to right itself, it seems like hours. The school's informal motto is: "You have to go out but you don't have to come back," meaning that when a life is in danger, they go out. No exceptions. As a testament to their training, very few men and women working on the lifeboats are ever injured.

Sometimes you can watch boats from the North Head lighthouse working in the surf as they go through their lifesaving drills. If they're working particularly close to the shore, where the surf is heaviest, you can also see them from the North Jetty of the river. Another viewpoint is from the Lewis and Clark Interpretive Center at the top of Cape Disappointment. It is wild and beautiful to watch the boats practicing in the heavy surf, sometimes being completely covered with a wave, and at other times riding atop the waves and crashing into shore.

The **Lewis and Clark Interpretive Center** was built to commemorate the arrival of the famous explorers in November 1805, the first overland party to cross America. Captain Meriwether Lewis had traveled from Washington, D.C., to meet the rest of the crew near St. Louis, which made him the first American to go overland from coast to coast. Originally the party intended to camp on the north side of the Columbia River, but when the travelers tried to set up camp they didn't like the exposed area, and forests that contained food on the hoof—deer and elk—were too far away. So they paddled across the river and settled on a site back in the woods on a small river where they had shelter from the winter storms and where deer and elk weren't so distant. The interpretive center tells the story of the expedition and offers one of the best views of the coast from its aerie high on the cape.

Although US 101 swings inland around Willapa Bay and misses the Long Beach Peninsula, this is one of the state's most popular beach areas and should not be missed. The peninsula has excellent hotels and inns, two or three of the better restaurants in the state, interesting historical towns such as Oysterville, several good artists who sell their work direct to the public, and an incredibly long beach with room for thousands of visitors. The southwest onshore wind is almost constant, so kite flying is one of the most popular activities. In addition to recreation, this area is also known for its cranberry bogs and oyster farms.

State WA 103 swings west off 101 just north of Ilwaco and goes almost all the way to the north end of the peninsula along the ocean side. (Sadly, its route stays almost entirely behind the high sand dunes that hide the coast, unless you follow the side roads that dead-end on the beaches. Near the top of the peninsula, WA 103 takes a hard right turn to Oysterville. A spur road leads due north to Leadbetter Point and the state park that bears the

same name. For the most part, **Leadbetter Point State Park** is beach, salt marshes and tidal flats. It is usually windy and not sheltered, and almost always wet. It is best known for the high and diverse bird population that includes black brant, Canada geese, canvasbacks, and snowy plover. Much of the point is flooded at high tide, and during most of the winter, so dress accordingly.

WA 103 enjoys several names as it meanders down the bay side of the peninsula, from Oysterville back to the starting point just north of Ilwaco. Don't worry about getting lost because there are only two north–south roads on the peninsula, and either will get you back to Start.

US 101 stays close to **Willapa Bay** most of the way north to South Bend and Raymond. The bay is shallow, and during low tide you will see miles and miles of mudflats with all manner of patterns created by the receding water and the small streams that enter the bay.

At Raymond the highway swings

Nearly all lighthouses are automated today, but they maintain their lonely vigil.

The almost constant breezes, or more likely, strong winds, make kite flying an obvious choice for visitors.   Long Beach Chamber of Commerce

inland through hilly country and forests that are mostly owned by timber companies. The highway occasionally has turnout lanes for logging trucks and recreational vehicles, but like most of US 101 the driving is best done at a modest speed.

If you want to follow the coastline all the way north, you can turn west in Raymond on WA 105, which will take you around the northern shore of Willapa Bay. From 105 a one-way road can take you south to Tokeland, where the Shoalwater Indians have a casino and the venerable, old Tokeland Hotel stands in its turn-of-the-twentieth-century splendor. From Tokeland, WA 105 continues around to Grayland and Westport on the Pacific coast, then swings back east along the shore of Grays Harbor to the tri-cities of Cosmopolis, Aberdeen, and Hoquiam. These towns are clustered around the eastern end of Grays Harbor, another large natural harbor that, until the spotted owl controversy, was one of the state's busiest ports for log exporting. The bay is sheltered from the ocean by peninsulas of sand that have built up over the centuries, while the middle of the entrance has been kept clear by water from rivers heading into the ocean. The southern peninsula features the commercial and sport-fishing and boat-building town of Westport, and the northern peninsula cradles the resort and summer-home community of Ocean Shores. Ocean Shores deserves a special mention here for one of the most unusual celebrations you're likely to hear of. It is called Undiscovery Day, which commemorates April 27, 1792, the day that Captain George Vancouver sailed past and did not discover Ocean Shores. The first observance of Undiscovery Day occurred when an enthusiastic group of local citizens met in the Horizon Room of the Inn; at midnight, in a mean wind, they walked out onto the beach, faced west into the open ocean, and yelled, "HEY, GEORGE!" The banner they held bore those same words. Their call was to the explorer Captain George Vancouver of the English Royal Navy, who sailed past the peninsula in the HMS *Discovery* on April 27, 1792, without detecting it.

US 101 doesn't show you much of the harbor and it leaves Hoquiam and heads north into the heart of the Olympic Peninsula, avoiding the coastal communities of Ocean Shores, Ocean City, Copalis Beach, Pacific Beach, and Moclips. The latter town is the farthest you can drive on WA 109 unless you are a member of the Quinault tribe or have special permission to enter the Quinault Reservation. Tired of encroachments by non-Native Americans, the Quinaults closed the Reservation beaches at the reservation boundary in the late 1960s and stopped issuing long-term property leases to people who were not members of the tribe. Visitors are welcomed on the beautiful reservation, but the beach visits are controlled. To see any of the beaches of the reservation, stop by the main Tribal Administrative building in Taholah on a weekday and ask for a day pass.

From Taholah northward, the highway is mostly an avenue through the forest. You'll first go through privately owned forest, then national forest land until you reach Lake Quinault on the southern edge of Olympic National Park. This large lake is the source of the Quinault River and has excellent fishing and boating. Lake Quinault Lodge is the most popular place on the lake, and it is one of those ancient wooden lodges that remind you of more gracious eras when cars that had to be cranked to start. It is a sister to Klaloch Lodge a short distance to the north and right on the ocean.

From Quinault Lake you can go back into the national park to trailheads that lead into the rain forest that is the ecological signature of the Olympic Peninsula. The temperate rain forest here is one of only three in the entire world (the others are in Chile and New Zealand), and it is an odd sensation to walk through the dense forest between and beneath trees virtually dripping with moss, yet in gentle temperatures that hover around 50 degrees. It is the silence of this forest that strikes visitors, in addition to the lush scenery, of course. If moss doesn't literally drip, the skies do. More than 200 inches (that's more than 16 feet) of rainfall is recorded here each year. Bring your rain gear.

The highway swings back to the west and reaches the coast eight miles later at Queets, a small village on the northern boundary of the Quinault Reservation. Here the coastal strip of Olympic National Park begins and continues north to La Push. This strip was controversial when it was added by President Franklin D. Roosevelt in the late 1930s, and still is controversial among those who would like to log all the timber of the peninsula. However, the national park has preserved the beach in its wild state, and one of the most popular hikes in the state is along the ocean beach. Some hikers complete the entire strip between where the highway leaves the beach at the Hoh River to Ozette, a distance of about 46 miles. Most hike it in two or three stages; hiking on the beaches is hard going if you have to walk in loose sand above the tideline with a heavy pack, and you must plan your hike around the tides to avoid being stranded on a headland or rock by the high tide.

This stretch of highway is one of the most beautiful in the state, and some travelers say it features the most dramatic scenery along the entire length of US 101, from California to Washington, although Oregonians might have something to say in the discussion since the highway follows its entire coastline. This stretch of Washington coast is very rugged, with hundreds of offshore rocks that are home for marine mammals and birds. The forest along here has never been logged, so most of it is the way nature designed it. Several trails lead from the highway down to the beach. Ruby Beach is a particular favorite with photographers. Other trails lead back into the main part of the national park, to the Hoh Rain Forest, and other points of interest.

After following the coast for a while, the highway heads back inland again at the Hoh River, then swings around north past the Bogachiel River State Park and along the bank of the Bogachiel River. The river is notable for its sea-run cutthroat trout and winter steelhead runs.

The next town is Forks, one of the state's most famous towns even though its population is only about three thousand. Forks is the ultimate logging town; until the emergence of the spotted owl as an indicator for loss of wildlife habitat, nearly everyone who lived in Forks was involved in

Marymere Falls is one of the prettiest waterfalls on the Olympic Peninsula.

Clam diggers often get caught up in the chase and go after the crafty bivalves with everything in their arsenal. Long Beach Chamber of Commerce

some way with logging. The decline in logging has forced its citizens to cast about for other sources of income, but their rugged individualism still thrives.

Forks has several legendary events and characters in its past, and my favorite is what happened when a famous motorcycle club arrived one holiday weekend, intent on taking over the town. The police were out-numbered and the town was too isolated to get immediate help from other sources. So the fire department was called out and it joined the police force in battling the bikers. They, too, were overwhelmed. The citizenry had enough of this nonsense, so dozens of loggers jumped in and helped evict the gang without worrying too much about the gang's civil rights. Soon US 101 was filled with motorcycles heading south. It wasn't as though the police never had trouble with the loggers. Some of the loggers had been thrown in jail by the police during various Friday or Saturday night brawls.

But this was different. "We don't like for our cops to get bent," was how one citizen described the reasoning behind joining the policemen and firemen in the brawl.

Nothing much happened in Forks over the years as the logging community struggled to survive during the ups and downs of the timber industry. It was too far inland and got too much rain (108 inches a year—that's nine feet) to be much of a travel destination. But in 2006, everything changed. The writer Stephanie Meyer, based in Phoenix, began writing a series of novels: a continuing saga of the adventures of a teenager named Bella and a handsome vampire named Edward. Meyer set her tales, collectively called the Twilight Saga, in Forks and the surrounding area. The first four books in the series sold more than 70 million copies worldwide.

"For my setting, I knew I needed someplace ridiculously rainy," Ms. Meyer explained on her Web site.

"I . . . looked for the place with the most rainfall in the U.S. This turned out to be the Olympic Peninsula in Washington State. I pulled up maps of the area and studied them, looking for something small, out of the way, surrounded by forest . . . And there, right where I wanted it to be, was a tiny town called 'Forks.' It couldn't have been more perfect if I had named it myself. . . . If the name hadn't sold me, the gorgeous photographs would have done the trick . . . In researching Forks, I discovered the La Push Reservation, home to the Quileute Tribe. The Quileute story is fascinating, and a few fictional members of the tribe quickly became intrinsic to my story."

Just like that, Forks became the rage as a place to visit. Washington hadn't seen anything like it since the TV series Northern Exposure used the old mining town of Roslyn in Eastern Washington as a backdrop. Forks is *the* destination for lovers of Ms. Meyer's novels, called the Twilight Saga. They call themselves Twihards and they have tripled the number of visitors the rain-soaked town has annually. As a Chamber of Commerce official said, in the past when she told someone she was from Forks, people would just stare. "Now when they hear where you're from, they're breathless."

A road leads from Forks down to the coastal town of La Push on the small Quillayute Indian Reservation. Quillayute has an excellent beach, and this is the entrance to the Quillayute Needles National Wildlife Refuge and the Washington Islands Wilderness Area. All offshore rocks along the coast are designated national wildlife refuges to provide habitat for birds and sea mammals. Consequently you cannot climb on them.

The campground at La Push is a good place to launch long hikes in

Beards Hollow is a favorite place for beachcombers to search for treasures from the ocean, and for people to go for walks with friends. Long Beach Chamber of Commerce

either direction. To the north is the spectacular Rialto Beach, and to the south are the unimaginatively named but beautiful Second and Third beaches. If you only want a good day hike, you can hike either direction to the first headland, climb it for a view of the coastline, then return to your car at La Push.

Shortly after leaving Forks, the highway takes a swing around to the east for its run through the forest to the small town of Sappho and continues on to Lake Crescent, which many consider the most beautiful lake on the Olympic Peninsula, if not in the entire state. Even though US 101 runs along its southern shore and logging trucks scare the bejesus out of dawdling tourists, the lake is surrounded by such beautiful mountains and there are so few developments on its shores (most of it is owned by the Olympic National Park) that it is very easy to forget that it isn't out in the wilderness alone.

Three lodges lie along the lake, and you will find several places to pull off the highway for a breather or short hike. One of the best views in the area is from atop Pyramid Peak on the northwestern shore, a hike that takes between two and three hours from the lake. During World War II an aircraft spotter station was built atop the peak, and from this perch you can see far back into the Olympics and north across the Strait of Juan de Fuca to Canada.

Another nice hike that will take less than an hour is to Marymere Falls, only a short distance from the highway on a fairly level trail. The highway skirts Lake Sutherland a short distance east of Crescent, then drops down into Port Angeles, the largest town on the peninsula. Here you can catch the ferry MIV Coho to Victoria, British Columbia, and you can stop in at the Olympic National Park headquarters on the edge of town. A good side trip is to Hurricane Ridge, which gives you a helicopter-like view into the heart of the Olympic Mountains and most of the Strait of Juan de Fuca with Vancouver Island and Victoria in the background.

The country-road aspect of US 101 disappears at Port Angeles. The traffic increases markedly and commercial development takes over from here to Hood Canal. It is interesting to note that only a short distance from where the annual rainfall is more than sixteen feet, you will cross through the rain-shadow effect at Sequim, where the Olympic Mountains rob nearly all the clouds of their rain, leaving only ten inches or less for the area in line with the rain-robbing peaks. This has made the small town of Sequim particularly attractive to retirees who want a mild climate without getting their feet wet. Several retirement homes and communities have sprung up around the small but rapidly growing town.

The highway next skirts the southern end of Discovery Bay, where WA 20 begins, and 101 heads almost due south along the western shore of **Hood Canal.** Several state parks and marinas are located along this stretch, but the traffic is so heavy that the silence of the forest is missing. Still, it is a beautiful drive with many places to turn off for walks and picnics in state parks, where you'll be safe from the territorial imperative that is so prevalent along Hood Canal.

After leaving Hood Canal, US 101 speeds along to Shelton, a sawmill town that has a beautiful setting on a long, narrow hook of Puget Sound called Hammersley Inlet. The area is perhaps best known for its Christmas tree industry. The soil in this area is not conducive to growing trees for lumber, but the poor soil produces small, hardy trees that are perfect for Christmas trees. So each winter more than 3 million trees are cut, packaged, and shipped all over America.

Before leaving this area, it is worth noting that politics in Washington are not much different from other states except that politeness isn't considered a sign of weakness. However, one incident from the pioneer days proves this concern for decorum was not always present in Olympia.

US 101 continues south from Shelton to vanish as it joins WA 8 at Mud Bay, shortly before WA 8 itself vanishes when it joins I-5 on the edge of the state capital, Olympia.

A GILBERT AND SULLIVAN PLOT

During Olympia's earliest days as Washington's capital, an incident occurred that today sounds as though Gilbert and Sullivan could have written it, even though no music has yet been composed. It involves Isaac Ingalls Stevens, the bantam-sized military man appointed the territory's first governor, and the territory's chief justice, Edward Lander, a man every bit as stubborn as Stevens.

Life was quite harsh for those who arrived first. They had to contend with the damp, cool-to-cold weather and the dark forest that came right down to the high-tide mark. This incident occurred during the winter of 1855–56, the so-called "blockhouse winter," when life was dangerous for everyone.

Little is known about Judge Lander and his career except that a street was named for him in Seattle. Much is known about Governor Stevens because he was a lightning rod for trouble during his tenure. Stevens, a New Englander, was very small—some speculate that he suffered a form of dwarfism—and brilliant. He built up an impressive resume before he arrived in the wilderness: a West Point graduate, he fought in the Mexican War, was assigned to the U.S. Coast Survey, and, because he had served well under General Franklin Pierce in Mexico, was one of several to receive political spoils. He was named governor of the newly created Washington Territory, superintendent of Indian Affairs, and commander of the Northern Pacific Railroad Survey, one of five such surveys intended to find a route from the Mississippi River to the Pacific Ocean.

None of his jobs was simple, and Stevens wasn't the most patient of men. He wanted everything done immediately, and his methods of rounding up Indian chiefs and getting them to sign treaties were accomplished with the finesse of a bogus aluminum siding salesman. He was basically honest, and never a hint of scandal touched him, but he wasn't always sensitive to the feelings of those around him.

One result of his treatment of the Indians was the hostilities that were to come. In the summer and fall of 1855 the troubles began, first from misunderstandings between the races, then outright hostilities, murders and burnings included. The settlers began banding together and converting churches and some large homes into blockhouses. Several blockhouses were built around the sound while the Indians destroyed many crops and either killed or stole whatever cattle they could find. Several families were killed in the process.

Governor Stevens called out the militia, of course, but they had a very difficult time catching the Indians because their strikes were without pattern and they did not care to stay and fight. Looking for someone to blame, some of the Americans noticed that the Indians did not touch the homes and farms of former Hudson's Bay employees (who were British), while all around them smoke flew from the burning homes and barns of American settlers. Nor did it go unnoticed that most of the British subjects were married to or living with Indian women.

When the militia questioned them, they said they were neutral and exempt from trouble with the Indians, but Stevens didn't believe them. Since they were now subject to the laws of America, he ordered them into the blockhouses with the other settlers. When they refused, Stevens ordered them arrested, and in order to do this he had to declare martial law in Pierce County. He announced that he would have them tried by a military court.

Immediately lawyers attempted to get the British released under writ of habeas corpus. The presiding judge of Pierce County was ill and the other judge available was Edward Lander, who was also commander of Company A in Seattle. He left his post to go down to Steilacoom to free the Englishmen, which made him vulnerable because he had left without permission from his commanding officer: Governor Stevens.

Judge Lander opened civil court in defiance of Stevens' proclamation that placed the county under martial law. Wasting no time with paperwork, Stevens sent a detachment of soldiers to arrest Lander for being AWOL. The judge and his court clerks were taken to Olympia, in Thurston County, home of Lander's courtroom. Stevens released Lander so he could open his regular court term, but, taking no chances, he declared Thurston County under martial law, too.

In the meantime, the settlers whose existence had caused all of this confusion were in jail, listening to rumors of the battle. To everyone's surprise, Stevens decided he had acted rashly and released three of the five men he had ordered arrested. The remaining two were to stand trial in a military court.

Lander made his next move. When his regular court term opened, Lander said the fact that it was in session proved it was functioning, so he immediately, perhaps gleefully, ordered the arrest of Governor Stevens for contempt of that court and sent a U.S. marshal to arrest him. When the marshal met Stevens face to face, the marshal looked down at the brilliant and determined little man, had second thoughts, and backed down. He returned to Olympia empty-handed.

Now even more furious, Stevens sent a militia into Olympia after Lander, who adjourned his court and ran for cover. The militia found him hiding in a friend's law office, kicked down the door, and placed him under arrest. He was taken to Fort Montgomery nearby and held in "honorable custody" until Stevens released him.

Equally angry and stubborn, Lander continued his case against the governor for contempt of court. To put an end to the whole thing, Stevens appeared in court by counsel and was fined $50.

Everyone thought the case was closed. Lander stayed out of the limelight, and Stevens went on to be killed in the second Battle of Chantilly in the Civil War. However, just after the turn of this century, while rummaging through old records in Olympia a clerk found a remarkable document signed by Stevens. It stated that Isaac I. Stevens, as governor, had pardoned Isaac I. Stevens, convicted of contempt of court. It was dated only a short time after he had paid the $50 fine.

IN THE AREA

This route is a long journey, covering nearly 400 miles, and probably worthy of a separate guidebook. Rather than listing every place to sleep and eat along the route, I have covered only the major tourist areas—the Long Beach Peninsula, the two grand old National Park lodges, and the eccentric town of Forks. Once you reach the Strait of Juan de Fuca and its large towns, and head south to the end of the route, you'll be in more urban settings. Most of the backroad flavor disappears after Forks.

Long Beach Peninsula

Long Beach Peninsula has one of the largest concentrations of inns, B&Bs, motels, restaurants, and cafes in the states, so please consider the list below a teaser, and visit the appropriate Web sites for more information.

Hurricane Ridge in Olympic National Park is one of the most popular places to drive on the Olympic Peninsula.

Accommodations

A Rendezvous Place Bed & Breakfast, 1610 California Ave. S, Long Beach. Call 360-642-8877 or 866-642-8877. Each of the five guest rooms is named for a flower the owners grow in the gardens surrounding the B&B. The entire place is sometimes rented to families or groups of friends. Web site: www.rendezvousplace.com.

The Breakers, 210 26th St. NW, Long Beach. Call 360-642-4414 or 800-219-9833. This large resort (125 units) is one of the peninsula's most popular. Rooms range from economy to multi-room suites.

China Beach Retreat, 222 Robert Gray Dr., Ilwaco. Call 360-642-5660 or 800-INN-1896. The inn has views across the mouth of the Columbia River and Baker Bay. Breakfast is served in the Shelburne Inn (see below).

Shelburne Inn, 4415 Pacific Way, Seaview. Call 360-642-2442 or 800-INN-1896. This century-old inn has the same owners as the China Beach Retreat. In addition to 15 rooms, this inn has a dining room that earned a four-star rating.

Dining

Café Akari, 203 Bolstad Ave., Long Beach. Call 360-642-3828. Open for all meals with an emphasis on seafood, the cafe also a wine and gift shop.

Bailey's Bakery & Café, 26910 Sandridge Rd., Nahcotta. Call 360-665-4449. Open for lunch only Thursday through Monday, Bailey's specializes in fresh breads and other baked goods.

42nd Street Café, 4201 Pacific Way, Seaview. Call 360-642-2323. One of the most popular eateries on the peninsula, 42nd Street specializes in what we might call gourmet comfort food.

From Long Beach to Forks

Accommodations

Lake Quinault Lodge, 345 South Shore Rd., P.O. Box 7, Quinault. Call 360-288-2900 or 800-562-6672. E-mail: info@visitlakequinault.com

Kalaloch Lodge, 157151 Hwy. 101, Forks. Call 360-962-2271 or 866-525-2562. This beautiful old lodge on the oceanfront has fallen in love with the Twilighters and offers a *New Moon–Twilight* package that involves a log cabin, dessert, and a *Twilight* water bottle. E-mail: info@visitkalaloch.com

Tokeland Hotel and Restaurant, 100 Hotel Rd., Tokeland. Call 360-267-7006. Each of the eighteen rooms in this turn-of-the-century classic is decorated with antiques. Web site: www.tokelandhotel.com

Forks

Accommodations

Dew Drop Inn Motel, 100 Fern Hill Rd., Forks. Call 360-374-4055. The blood-red Bella Suite is the inn's major attraction, and it comes with sparkling cider and chocolates. Web site: www.dewdropinnmotel.com

Pacific Inn Motel, 352 South Forks Ave., Forks. Call 800-235-7344. Six of these rooms have the *Twilight* theme. Web site: www.pacificinnmotel .com

Other Contacts

Forks Visitor Information Center, 1411 S. Forks Ave., Forks. Call 360-443-6757. Web site: www.forkswa.com

Grays Harbor Chamber of Commerce, 506 Duffy St., Aberdeen. Call 360-532-1924. Web site: www.graysharbor.org

Long Beach Peninsula Association, 3914 Pacific Way (Hwy 101 at Hwy 103), Seaview. Call 360-642-2400 or 800-451-2542. Web site: www .funbeach.com

Olympic National Park, 600 East Park Ave., Port Angeles. Call 360-565-3000.

Port Angeles Chamber of Commerce, 121 E. Railroad Ave., Port Angeles. Call 360-452-2363. Web site: www.portangeles.org

Sequim Chamber of Commerce, 1192 E. Washington St., Sequim. Call 360-683-6197. Web site: www.sequimchamber.com

Shelton Chamber of Commerce, 21 W. Railroad Ave., Shelton. Call 360-426-2021. Web site: www.sheltonchamber.org

Quinault Tribal Administration, 1214 Aalis Dr., P.O. Box 189, Taholah. Call 360-276-8215, ext. 208 or 309.

This view of Dewatto shows Hood Canal and the Olympic National Forest.

CHAPTER

17

Inside Hood Canal

Estimated length: 52 miles
Estimated time: 2 hours

Getting there: From WA 3 in Belfair, turn west on WA 300 toward Belfair State Park and Tahuya. Then watch for signs on the unnumbered county roads north to Holly, Seabeck, and Silverdale.

Highlights: You'll see the eastern shore of Hood Canal, with grand views across the narrow saltwater arm of the Olympic Mountains, and villages ranging from tiny to small.

In no place in Washington is the property-ownership impulse—perhaps the "territorial imperative" would be more accurate—more rampant than along the shores of Hood Canal. More PRIVATE PROPERTY signs are posted along this stretch of waterfront than in any other place I have ever visited. These people simply do not want you walking on their turf and you have no choice but to take them seriously. Argue with them and assorted law-enforcement officers are likely to descend on you. Unlike Oregon and a few other enlightened states, Washington permits people to own beaches and tidelands, and most of these owners are protective of their property to the extreme.

Example: A few years ago a friend and I packed a picnic lunch and drove down Hood Canal looking for a likely place to park our hamper and enjoy the sun, light breeze, and views. We found a tideflat with a place to park beside the road, a well-used trail, and no PRIVATE PROPERTY signs. We had our picnic laid out on a stump, the wine opened, and the potato salad sampled when a woman with a serious expression and a notebook came down the trail and demanded our names. "I already have your license number," she said, "so you had just as well give me your names because I can get them anyway." We didn't give her our names, but we did leave. You can enjoy Hood Canal without getting into territorial disputes by sticking to the obviously public areas, such as Belfair State Park, and designated picnic areas in the towns along the route.

Hood Canal is not actually a canal. It is an 80-mile-long arm of Puget Sound with a sharp hook on the southern end. It comes awfully close to meeting the rest of Puget Sound at its very tip; there are no more than two miles between the canal and the northern tip of Case Inlet. You can rest assured that if it had been commercially practical, or if it ever will be, a real canal will be built. Although its narrow configuration might lead you to think it was mistaken for a canal by the explorers, it was named Hood's Channel by Captain George Vancouver in 1792 in honor of Lord Hood of the Admiralty Board. Someone entered it on Vancouver's charts as Hood's Canal, and eventually it became Hood Canal. Nobody seems to know why.

Although it is easiest to find public places along US 101, my favorite trip along the canal is along the shoreline on the inside of the hook. This route is less traveled, and the road is unpaved much of the way.

At Belfair on WA 3, turn west on WA 300 toward Belfair State Park and Tahuya. The road is busy during the summer months because Belfair State Park is very popular. If you didn't buy your picnic supplies in Belfair, you can stop at the store across the road from the state park. This will be your last chance for food or gasoline until you reach Holly.

The road stays close to the shore most of the way to Tahuya with peek-a-boo views of the salt water through the houses and trees. The road is generally slow because it is crooked and nobody is in a hurry, anyway. The canal has its own special beauty, especially on the quiet mornings when a fog hangs over it until the sun burns it off. On these mornings there is no wind to ruffle the surface. Birds create perfect reflections as they fly only inches off the water, and a jumping fish makes almost as much noise as a beaver slapping its tail on the water.

Not until you reach **Tahuya** will the views be really spectacular, because that is where the Olympics make their appearance. Tahuya is a very small town, and if you ask around you will probably find a place to picnic without threat of arrest.

Just after you leave town, the timber is so dense that you'll feel as though you're entering a cave. From here to Dewatto you are driving on a country road: steep in places, narrow most of the time, and muddy in wet weather. You'll find a few wide spots where you can pull over to the side and admire the views. But even though you are away from the water, and in places several hundred feet above sea level, you'll still be greeted by PRIVATE PROPERTY signs.

After about eight miles of driving up and down and around sharp curves, you will find that the road drops back down to relatively level land and is in a bit better condition. Then it abruptly reaches a T-junction. Turn left and you'll soon be on the tideflats of Dewatto Creek. Turn left at the road by the creek bridge and it will lead you down to the almost-ghost-town of Dewatto, a place being constantly rediscovered by people wanting a rural experience.

The place was named by the local Native Americans, who didn't like it at all. They avoided it and called it Du-a-ta, meaning "place where the evil spirits come out of the earth." They believed these spirits, named Tub-ta-ba, entered people's bodies and drove them crazy. Some antidevelopment folks would probably like for the stories to be resurrected.

Beyond Dewatto the road leaves the shore again and climbs out of the old-growth timberland into an area that was logged off many years ago. The first time I drove this road, in 1979, the new trees weren't much larger than a standard Christmas tree. A decade later the trees are a forest, still not large enough to be cut but large enough to remind us what an emotional issue logging is, even when it occurs on private property. No matter how hard timber companies try to convince the public that trees are a crop (and let's be honest, they are), few of us can equate trees with corn and peas and boysenberries. As the philosopher said, "Go figure."

After climbing gradually for several miles on the washboardlike road, which feels sunken because the banks on either side are so high and the trees are now so tall, you'll finally reach the crest and begin an ascent toward the saltwater again. At the bottom of the hill, turn left for Holly, a small town that was once quite remote, a popular place for summer homes. Today it's part of the suburbia that is creeping across the Kitsap Peninsula and around Hood Canal. From here, the highway takes you to Seabeck and Puget Sound.